MEAL PREP AIR FRYER

SUPER HEALTHY MEALS IN MINUTES

Max McCann
@mealswithmax

MEAL PREP AIR FRYER

SUPER HEALTHY MEALS IN MINUTES

Max McCann
@mealswithmax

Contents

Introduction	6
Using your Portable Air Fryer	8
Meal Prep Tips	9
Meal Plans and Shopping Lists	10
How to Use This Book	14

01	**Breakfast**	16
02	**Chicken**	32
03	**Beef**	48
04	**Pork**	64
05	**Fish**	80
06	**Vegetarian**	96
07	**Vegan**	112
08	**Fakeaways**	128
09	**Snacks**	144
10	**Sweet Treats**	160

Conversion Tables	176
Index	178
About the Author	188
Acknowledgements	190

Introduction

I started cooking when I was just three years old, standing on a stool in the kitchen helping my mum prep dinners. My dad was a chef his whole life, so food has always been part of our family. I didn't realise it at the time, but those early moments of peeling veg and stirring sauces shaped how much I love cooking today.

For me, cooking has never been about spending hours making something complicated – it's about food that tastes great, brings people together and fits into real life. I know what it's like to get home tired and hungry, and not want to spend ages in the kitchen. That's why I'm obsessed with finding ways to cook meals that are quick, cheap and genuinely delicious.

That's exactly what this book is all about. Every recipe in here is under 500 calories, so you can eat well without feeling restricted. They're simple enough for busy weekdays, but tasty enough to actually look forward to. All the recipes have been written and tested using the Ninja Crispi (but will work well with similar devices); it's compact and easy to clean, and with the glass dishes you can cook one-portion meals or reheat food without it ever going soggy. Honestly, it's become my favourite tool in the kitchen.

The recipes in this book really show what these portable air fryers can do. The Chorizo and Sweet Potato Hash (see page 26) is hearty, colourful and the kind of meal that works any time of day. The Harissa Chicken with Chickpeas, Courgette and Crispy Potatoes (see page 34) is bold, filling and packed with flavour. And if you're craving a fakeaway vibe, the Sweet Chilli Halloumi and Red Pepper Burger (see page 142) is a proper crowd-pleaser. Of course, balance matters too – which is why I had to include the Chocolate Lava Cake (see page 164). It's rich and gooey, and proves you can enjoy a treat without throwing off your routine.

You don't need a fancy kitchen or loads of gadgets for any of this. All you really need is your air fryer, and the confidence to give it a go. I've organised the book by protein because, let's be honest, that's how most of us think about dinner: chicken, fish, beef, veggie? But nothing's set in stone. Don't eat meat? Swap chicken for vegan pieces, or try beans and lentils instead. Cooking should be flexible – these recipes are here to guide you, not limit you.

Most of all, I want this book to give you confidence. Play with the flavours, make swaps and have fun with it. That's how I learned – watching my parents cook, making mistakes and trying again.

If you cook something you're proud of, I'd love to see it. Please share your creations with me on Instagram, TikTok or YouTube and tag me @mealswithmax. Cooking is always better when it's shared, and I can't wait to see what you come up with.

INTRODUCTION

Using your Portable Air Fryer

MEAL PREP MADE EASY

Portable glass air fryers like the Ninja Crispi and the Kismile Roasti come with two glass containers (and you can buy more if you need them). These containers can be used to store the food as well as cook it, so you can prepare your traybake in advance. That way, all you need to do at dinner time is attach the power pod and set the timer.

The three settings

Air fry Your go-to for chips, chicken, fish, veg ... basically anything you want golden and crunchy.

Roast Steady, even heat. Great for meat, roasted veg or anything you'd usually stick in the oven.

Recrisp The secret weapon. Last night's pizza, fries or wings come back tasting brand new instead of sad and soggy.

Portable air fryers

The reset quirk On the Ninja Crispi. if you lift the power pod, it automatically jumps back to Air Fry mode. Handy to know if you were using Roast or Recrisp, as you'll need to flick it back over.

Cold food takes longer Cooking food straight from the fridge? Add a couple of minutes to the cooking time, as the device must warm up the dish as well as the food.

Preheat hack You don't usually need to, but if you want super crisp results, run it empty for 1–2 minutes before adding your food.

Don't overcrowd it Spread food out in a single layer where you can. If you pile it in, it won't cook evenly.

Shake it up Halfway through cooking, give the dish a shake or flip things over. This simple trick makes a big difference.

Light oil = better crisp A quick spray of oil on the glass dish (or directly on the food) helps things crisp and stop sticking.

Let the air circulate Use the plastic tray in the glass dish for even crispier results.

Experiment Portable air fryers aren't just for chips and chicken. Try snacks, fakeaways and even desserts (yes, sweet treats like the Cinnamon Oat Apple Crumble on page 170 work perfectly in here).

Meal Prep Tips

Here are my top tips for meal prepping and food safety:

Cool it first Don't put hot food straight in the fridge. Let it cool down first or you'll heat up everything else in there.

One reheat only Cook it once, reheat it once. Heating the same meal over and over makes it less tasty and less safe.

Trust your senses If it smells weird, looks dodgy or you're second-guessing it …don't risk it. Bin it.

Piping hot is the rule When reheating, make sure it's steaming all the way through. Warm in the middle isn't good enough.

Label your tubs Write the date on containers so you actually know what's what. Saves you from 'mystery meal roulette' later in the week.

Know your limits As a rule of thumb, go for 3 days in the fridge, up to 3 months in the freezer, unless stated otherwise in the recipe.

Freeze smart Cool food fully before freezing. Portion it out so you can defrost just what you need.

Plan your week A quick meal plan saves you time, money and stress. Plus, you'll know exactly what to buy when you go shopping. To get you started, I've put together a couple of weekly meal plans and their shopping lists on pages 10–13.

Batch the basics Roast a tray of veggies, cook up some grains or prep chicken ahead. You can mix and match these into loads of different meals.

Stack your fridge right Keep raw meat at the bottom (so nothing drips on your other food) and put the ready-to-eat stuff up top.

Don't overcrowd your fridge Cold air needs to circulate. If you've crammed it full, food won't chill properly.

Portion for grab-and-go Store meals in single portions so you can just grab one, heat and eat.

Glass or BPA-free tubs Airtight containers keep food fresher and stop smells from spreading. The containers that come with the Ninja Crispi are BPA free!

Cook for balance, not boredom Mix proteins, carbs and plenty of veg so you don't end up eating the same thing every day.

Meal Plans and Shopping Lists

MEAL PLAN - WEEK ONE

	BREAKFAST	LUNCH	DINNER
MONDAY	Apple Pie Baked Oats	Cherry Tomato, Feta and Basil Pasta Bake	Harissa Chicken with Chickpeas, Courgette and Crispy Potatoes
TUESDAY	Bacon and Egg Breakfast Bites	BBQ Jackfruit Wrap with Slaw and Pickles	Sweet and Sour Chicken with Rice
WEDNESDAY	Avocado, Halloumi and Tomato Sourdough Toast	Crispy Gnocchi with Tomatoes and Pesto	Hot Honey Chicken Burger
THURSDAY	Chorizo and Sweet Potato Hash	Moroccan-spiced Veg Tray with Chickpeas and Apricots	Loaded Beef Nachos
FRIDAY	Courgette, Red Onion and Goat's Cheese Frittata	Indian Paneer and Pepper Bake with Coriander Chutney	Sweet Chilli Halloumi and Red Pepper Burger
SATURDAY	Cinnamon French Toast with Frozen Berries and Yogurt	Crispy BBQ Chicken Wings with Ranch Dip	Thai-inspired Chicken Satay with Rice
SUNDAY	Sausage and Cheese Breakfast Muffin	Mexican Beef and Black Bean Tacos	Chilli Lemon Salmon with Corn Salsa and Zesty Rice

SHOPPING LIST - WEEK ONE

Fruit and Veg

- 1 apple
- bag of frozen mixed berries
- 2 lemons
- 5 limes
- 1 avocado
- 500g/1lb 2oz cherry tomatoes
- 5 red peppers
- 1 yellow pepper
- 3 courgettes
- 4 red onions
- 1 small onion
- 2 spring onions
- 160g/5½oz red cabbage
- 2 carrots
- 120g/4oz bag of baby spinach
- 1 lettuce
- 1 tomato
- fresh basil
- fresh coriander
- fresh chives
- bulb of garlic
- 1 green chilli
- small piece of fresh ginger

Protein and Dairy

- 17 eggs
- 250g/9oz Greek yogurt
- 250g/9oz halloumi
- 50g/1¾oz goat's cheese
- 200g/7oz paneer
- 190g/6½oz Cheddar
- 50g/1¾oz Parmesan
- 70g/2½oz feta
- 2 slices of burger cheese
- milk
- soured cream
- butter
- 1kg/2¼lb chicken breast
- 280g/10oz skinless and boneless chicken thighs
- 360g/12½oz chicken wings
- 2 salmon fillets
- 500g/1lb 2oz beef mince
- 100g/3½oz chorizo
- 4 sausages
- 4 rashers of bacon
- 250g/9oz tinned jackfruit

Carbs

- 100g/3½oz rolled oats
- loaf of sourdough
- 2 English muffins
- 120g/4oz fusilli pasta
- 220g/8oz basmati rice
- pouch of microwaveable basmati rice
- 2 tortilla wraps
- 4 small tortilla wraps
- 4 burger buns
- bag of tortilla chips
- 500g/1lb 2oz Maris Piper potatoes
- 700g/1½lb sweet potatoes
- 250g/9oz gnocchi

Pantry

- honey
- vanilla extract
- olive oil
- oil spray
- pesto
- pineapple juice
- pickled gherkins
- jalapeños
- harissa paste
- peanut butter
- salsa
- 250g/9oz passata
- 150g/5¼oz tinned tomatoes
- 200g/7oz tinned sweetcorn
- 250g/9oz tinned chickpeas
- 70g/2½oz tinned black beans
- dried apricots
- tomato ketchup
- tomato purée
- mayonnaise
- BBQ sauce
- sweet chilli sauce
- rice vinegar
- apple cider vinegar
- white vinegar
- soy sauce
- smoked paprika
- ground cinnamon
- ground cumin
- ground coriander
- ground turmeric
- garam masala
- curry powder
- garlic powder
- garlic granules
- onion powder
- dried dill
- dried parsley
- chilli flakes
- chilli powder
- cornflour
- baking powder
- icing sugar
- salt
- black pepper

Meal Plans and Shopping Lists

MEAL PLAN - WEEK TWO

	BREAKFAST	LUNCH	DINNER
MONDAY	Apple Pie Baked Oats	Sticky Korean Sesame Chicken Strips	Beef Kofta Salad with Spiced Chickpeas and Mint Yogurt Sauce
TUESDAY	Bacon and Egg Breakfast Bites	Baked Ricotta and Spinach Pasta with a Crispy Cheesy Crust	Lemon Garlic Chicken Thighs with Green Beans and Baby Potatoes
WEDNESSDAY	Avocado, Halloumi and Tomato Sourdough Toast	Mexican Chicken Burrito Bowl	Greek Beef Meatballs with Courgette, Feta and Lemon Rice
THURSDAY	Chorizo and Sweet Potato Hash	Moroccan-spiced Veg Tray with Chickpeas and Apricots	Cajun Cod with Spinach, Roasted Peppers and Turmeric Rice
FRIDAY	Courgette, Red Onion and Goat's Cheese Frittata	BBQ Pork Tacos with Coleslaw	Sausage and Veg Traybake with a Sticky Maple Glaze
SATURDAY	Cinnamon French Toast with Frozen Berries and Yogurt	Crispy Mozzarella Sticks with Marinara Sauce	Crispy Chilli Beef with Rice
SUNDAY	Sausage and Cheese Breakfast Muffin	Salt and Pepper Chicken	Chicken Katsu Curry with Rice

SHOPPING LIST - WEEK TWO

Fruit and Veg

1 apple
bag of frozen mixed berries
8 lemons
2 limes
2 courgettes
400g/14oz sweet potatoes
4 red onions
3 onions
6 spring onions
1 green pepper
6 red peppers

1 yellow pepper
2 red chillies
410g/14¼oz green beans
4 carrots
80g/3oz white cabbage
1 baby gem lettuce
200g/7oz cherry tomatoes
1 avocado
bag of baby spinach
bag of mixed salad leaves
½ cucumber

500g/1lb 2oz rice
2 bulbs of garlic
small piece of fresh ginger
fresh coriander
fresh parsley
fresh mint
fresh basil
fresh chives

Protein and Dairy

250g/9oz Greek yogurt
23 eggs
60g/2oz light halloumi
50g/1¾oz goat's cheese
120g/4oz mozzarella
40g/1½oz grated mozzarella
50g/1¾oz Parmesan
150g/5¼oz ricotta

50g/1¾oz Cheddar
50g/1¾oz feta
2 slices of burger cheese
milk
butter
soured cream
8 sausages
4 rashers of bacon
100g/3½oz chorizo

500g/1lb 2oz beef mince
1.5kg/3lb chicken breast
500g/1lb 2oz skinless and boneless chicken thighs
400g/14oz cod fillets
220g/8oz sirloin steak
320g/11½oz pork fillet

Carbs

100g/3½oz rolled oats
loaf of sourdough
2 English muffins
120g/4oz penne pasta
220g/8oz basmati rice

3 pouches of microwaveable basmati rice
pack of small tortilla wraps

160g/5½oz panko breadcrumbs
550g/1¼lb baby potatoes

Pantry

marinara sauce
200g/7oz passata
100g/3½oz tinned chickpeas
chicken stock
olive oil
oil spray
sesame oil
plain flour
cornflour
baking powder
icing sugar
vanilla extract
honey

light and dark soy sauce
rice vinegar
apple cider vinegar
balsamic vinegar
sweet chilli sauce
tomato ketchup
BBQ sauce
light mayonnaise
Dijon mustard
wholegrain mustard
gochujang
ground cumin
smoked paprika
ground turmeric

curry powder
Cajun seasoning
ground coriander
ground cinnamon
onion powder
garlic powder
garlic granules
chilli flakes
sesame seeds
Chinese five spice
dried thyme
dried oregano
salt
black pepper

How to Use This Book

This book is designed to make healthy cooking simple. Here's how to get the most out of it:

Follow the steps Every recipe is written to be clear and easy. Just follow along and you'll be fine, even if you're new to cooking. Look out for the 'Meals with Max Tips' for extra advice on cooking techniques, meal prep, reheating and storage throughout. These are the shortcuts I use every day.

Prep ahead A little batch cooking goes a long way. Many recipes can be made in advance and stored for busy days.

Reheat with confidence Portable air fryers like the Ninja Crispi make leftovers taste freshly cooked again. Always reheat until piping hot and check the notes for safe storage times.

Stay flexible Swap proteins, switch up veg or add extra spices. The recipes are here to guide you, not box you in. Use the meal plans if you want structure or just dip into whatever recipe you fancy.

Enjoy it This is the most important tip! Cooking isn't about being perfect – it's about making food that tastes good and works for you.

Breakfast is where the day starts right – and the air fryer makes it easy to keep things quick, clean and satisfying. Whether you're after something hearty like a Courgette, Red Onion and Goat's Cheese Frittata (page 24) or something light and crispy to grab on the go like the Bacon and Egg Breakfast Bites (page 28), these recipes prove mornings don't have to be boring. They come together fast, so you can still enjoy a proper breakfast even on busy mornings. My favourite recipe from this section is the Chorizo and Sweet Potato Hash (page 26) – it's smoky, filling and the perfect way to kick off the day.

Apple Pie Baked Oats	18
Cinnamon French Toast with Frozen Berries and Yogurt	20
Sausage and Cheese Breakfast Muffin	22
Courgette, Red Onion and Goat's Cheese Frittata	24
Chorizo and Sweet Potato Hash	26
Bacon and Egg Breakfast Bites	28
Avocado, Halloumi and Tomato Sourdough Toast	30

Breakfast

01

Apple Pie Baked Oats

If you love dessert for breakfast, this one is for you. These baked oats taste just like apple pie, with sweet cinnamon, soft baked apple and a golden top. It feels indulgent, but is actually really wholesome and filling. I make this when I've got a bit more time in the morning, or even prep it the night before and warm it up.

SERVES 2

Cook time: 20 minutes

INGREDIENTS:
100g/3½oz rolled oats
1 tsp baking powder
2 tsp ground cinnamon
2 eggs
160g/5½oz Greek yogurt
2 tbsp honey
1 tsp vanilla extract
4 tbsp milk
1 apple, peeled and finely diced
salt
butter, for greasing

METHOD:
1. Lightly grease the large glass dish of the portable air fryer with butter.
2. In a bowl, mix the oats, baking powder, cinnamon and a big pinch of salt.
3. Stir in the eggs, yogurt, honey, vanilla extract and milk. Then fold in most of the diced apple, saving a small amount for topping.
4. Pour the mixture into the prepared dish, without the tray, and top with the remaining apple.
5. Cook on the Roast setting for 12–14 minutes, or until golden brown on the top and set in the centre.
6. Let it cool for a few minutes before removing from the air fryer dish and serving, then enjoy. Lovely!

STORE: Cool completely and seal the glass dish with the lid, then store in the fridge for up to 3 days.

REHEAT: You can eat this hot or cold! To reheat, remove the lid and attach the portable air fryer. Use the Recrisp function to heat for 4–5 minutes, or until hot.

PREP AND GO: To prep this ahead of time, follow the above instructions to the end of step 4 and then attach the storage lid. Store in the fridge for up to 3 days. Once ready to cook, attach to the portable air fryer and continue from step 5.

MEALS WITH MAX TIPS:
- Feel free to mix up the toppings – chopped hazelnuts and raisins work great with this!
- If you are cooking for one, halve the ingredients and cook this in the smaller dish.

One Pot

● **Calories:** 442　　● **Protein:** 23g　　● **Carbs:** 67g　　● **Fat:** 11g

Cinnamon French Toast with Frozen Berries and Yogurt

French toast is such a classic, and this version is lightened up but still feels like a weekend treat. Cooking this in the portable air fryer makes it golden and crisp on the outside, while the cinnamon adds warmth and sweetness. Topping it with frozen berries and creamy yogurt keeps it fresh and balanced – it's one of my favourite ways to do a sweet breakfast.

SERVES 1

Cook time: 15 minutes

INGREDIENTS:
1 egg
75ml/5 tbsp milk
1 tsp vanilla extract
1 tbsp honey
1 tsp ground cinnamon
2 slices of thick bread
1 tbsp Greek yogurt
handful of frozen berries
icing sugar, for dusting

METHOD:
1. In a bowl, whisk together the egg, milk, vanilla extract, honey and cinnamon until fully combined.
2. Dip the bread slices into the egg mixture briefly, just enough to coat them. Don't let them soak in the mixture too long.
3. Place the coated bread into the large glass dish of the portable air fryer, on top of the tray.
4. Air fry for 10–12 minutes until golden and crispy, flipping carefully halfway through the cooking time.
5. Serve topped with a dollop of Greek yogurt and a handful of frozen berries. Dust with icing sugar and enjoy. Lovely!

STORE: Cool the French toast completely and seal the glass dish with the lid, then store in the fridge for up to 2 days. Don't add the toppings until serving.

REHEAT: Remove the lid and attach the portable air fryer. Use the Recrisp function to heat for 4–5 minutes, or until hot and crispy. Then add the berries and yogurt when serving.

MEALS WITH MAX TIPS:
- Don't leave the bread in the egg mixture for too long! This will cause it to go too soggy. Just dip in briefly until it fully coats the bread on both sides.
- If you prefer, you could swap the frozen berries for fresh berries.
- For a lower calorie option, use low-fat milk and 0% fat Greek yogurt.
- If you are cooking more than one portion, it is best to cook this in batches rather than squeeze too many slices of French toast into the air fryer at once.

One Pot

Calories: 446   **Protein:** 19g   **Carbs:** 73g   **Fat:** 9g

PREP + GO

SERVES 2

Cook time: 15 minutes

INGREDIENTS:
4 sausages
oil spray
2 slices of burger cheese
2 English muffins
tomato ketchup

Sausage and Cheese Breakfast Muffin

This is my healthier take on the classic sausage and cheese muffin – the kind you'd grab from a café. Cooking it in the portable air fryer gives the sausage patties a lovely crisp texture, and the melted cheese brings it all together in a soft toasted muffin. It's a proper treat for breakfast, but much lighter than the fast-food version.

METHOD:
1. Slice down the side of the sausages and remove the sausage meat from the skins.
2. Roll the sausage meat into two balls and then squash each ball flat to shape into a patty.
3. Place into the large glass dish of the portable air fryer, on top of the tray.
4. Spray with a little oil and air fry for 10–12 minutes, flipping halfway through the cooking time.
5. Slice the muffins in half and toast them in the air fryer for 2 minutes, or pop them in the toaster. Add a slice of burger cheese on top of each sausage patty for the final minute of cooking.
6. Spread ketchup on the bottom half of each muffin, add a sausage patty to each and place the top half of the bun on top. Serve and enjoy.

STORE: Cool the sausage patties completely and seal the glass dish with the lid, then store in the fridge for up to 3 days. If prepping ahead, it's best to not add the cheese or assemble if storing.

REHEAT: Remove the lid and attach the portable air fryer. Use the Recrisp function to heat the patties for 7–8 minutes, or until hot. Add the cheese for the final minute.

PREP AND GO: To prep this ahead of time, follow the above instructions to the end of step 3 and then attach the storage lid. Store in the fridge for up to 3 days. Once ready to cook, attach to the air fryer and continue from step 4.

MEALS WITH MAX TIPS:
- For a larger portion, double up the sausage patty and cheese!
- You could add bacon, or even swap the sausage for bacon.
- If you are cooking for one, halve the ingredients and cook this in the smaller dish.

One Pot

● **Calories:** 415　　● **Protein:** 22g　　● **Carbs:** 39g　　● **Fat:** 20g

Courgette, Red Onion and Goat's Cheese Frittata

I love how simple and versatile a frittata is, and this one is full of flavour from the sweet red onion, soft courgette and tangy goat's cheese. It's a great option if you want something high in protein that you can make ahead to enjoy for breakfast or even lunch. I often make extra, slice it up and keep it in the fridge for a couple of days – it reheats perfectly in the portable air fryer.

SERVES 2
Cook time: 15 minutes

INGREDIENTS:
½ tsp olive oil
6 eggs
big pinch of smoked paprika
60g/2oz baby spinach, roughly chopped
½ courgette, thinly sliced in half-moons
½ red onion, thinly sliced
50g/1¾oz soft goat's cheese, crumbled
salt and black pepper
basil leaves, to garnish

METHOD:
1. Lightly grease the large glass dish of the portable air fryer with the oil.
2. In a small bowl, whisk the eggs with the smoked paprika and some salt and black pepper. Stir in the chopped spinach, courgette and red onion. Pour the mixture directly into the greased glass dish, without the tray.
3. Attach the portable air fryer to the dish and cook on the Roast setting for 10–12 minutes, or until the eggs are set, stirring halfway through the cooking time to ensure even cooking.
4. Sprinkle over the goat's cheese and cook for a further 2 minutes.
5. Slide it out carefully from the dish and serve garnished with fresh basil leaves.

STORE: Cool completely, seal the glass dish with the lid, then store in the fridge for up to 2 days.

REHEAT: Remove the lid and attach the portable air fryer. Use the Recrisp function to heat for 4–5 minutes, or until hot throughout.

MEALS WITH MAX TIPS:
- Smoked paprika adds lovely depth and flavour, but you could swap it for some ground cumin to add a subtle warmth.
- Got leftover roasted veggies? Toss them in this to mix it up! It can help reduce waste – and bulk this out – without extra prep.
- If you are cooking for one, halve the ingredients and cook this in the smaller dish.

One Pot

Calories: 355 **Protein:** 27g **Carbs:** 11g **Fat:** 24g

PREP + GO

Chorizo and Sweet Potato Hash

This is the ultimate weekend breakfast – you can't beat those crispy edges! It's hearty, comforting and has just the right amount of spice to wake you up. I love topping it with a fried egg and digging straight in. It feels indulgent but is still balanced and packed with flavour.

SERVES 2

Cook time: 25 minutes

INGREDIENTS:
- 400g/14oz sweet potato, peeled and cut into 1cm/½in cubes
- 1 red pepper, diced
- 100g/3½oz chorizo, diced
- 2 tsp olive oil
- 1 tsp smoked paprika
- 60g/2oz baby spinach
- 2 eggs
- salt and black pepper

METHOD:
1. Place the diced sweet potato, red pepper and chorizo into a small bowl. Add 1 teaspoon of the olive oil, the smoked paprika and some salt and black pepper. Mix until everything is fully coated.
2. Place the veg and chorizo into the large glass dish of the portable air fryer, on top of the tray.
3. Air fry 18 minutes, stirring halfway through the cooking time.
4. Add the spinach, mix well, and air fry for a further 2 minutes.
5. Heat a small frying pan over a medium heat, add the remaining olive oil and crack in the eggs. Fry the eggs for 2–3 minutes.
6. Divide the sweet potato and chorizo hash between two plates or bowls and top each portion with a fried egg.

STORE: Cool the hash completely, seal the glass dish with the lid, then store in the fridge for up to 2 days. Cook the eggs when reheating.

REHEAT: Remove the lid and attach the portable air fryer. Use the Recrisp function to heat for 5–6 minutes, or until hot throughout.

PREP AND GO: To prep this ahead of time, follow the above instructions to the end of step 2 and then attach the storage lid. Store in the fridge for up to 3 days. Once ready to cook, attach to the portable air fryer and continue from step 3. You can't prep the eggs in advance; fry these during the final 2 minutes of cooking.

MEALS WITH MAX TIPS:
- Want it spicy? Sprinkle over some chilli flakes or drizzle with chilli oil to serve. Top with a dollop of Greek yogurt or smashed avocado for extra richness.
- If you are cooking for one, halve the ingredients and cook this in the smaller dish.

Calories: 489   **Protein:** 22g   **Carbs:** 46g   **Fat:** 25g

BREAKFAST

Bacon and Egg Breakfast Bites

These little bites are one of my go-tos for busy mornings. You get all the flavours of a cooked breakfast – bacon, eggs and cheese – but in a portable, bite-sized form. They're quick to prep and great for meal prep too. I often make a batch and keep them in the fridge, so I can grab a couple on the way out the door.

SERVES 2

Cook time: 25 minutes

INGREDIENTS:
4 rashers of bacon
6 eggs
50g/1¾oz Cheddar, grated
oil spray
salt and black pepper
chopped chives, to garnish
Ketchup, to serve (optional)

METHOD:
1. Place the bacon in the large glass dish of the portable air fryer, on top of the tray, and air fry for 10 minutes, or until crispy.
2. Remove the bacon from the air fryer, then chop into small pieces and set aside.
3. In a bowl, whisk the eggs, then stir in the cooked bacon, grated cheese, salt and black pepper.
4. Lightly grease four silicone muffin cases with oil spray, then pour in the egg mixture, filling each about three-quarters full.
5. Air fry for 10–12 minutes, or until puffed up and fully set in the centre.
6. Leave to cool for a minute before moving – they'll deflate slightly but stay fluffy inside.
7. Garnish with chopped chives, then serve and enjoy.

STORE: Cool completely, seal the glass dish with the lid, then store in the fridge for up to 3 days.

REHEAT: You can eat these hot or cold! To reheat, remove the lid and attach the portable air fryer. Use the Recrisp function to heat for 3–4 minutes, or until hot throughout.

MEALS WITH MAX TIPS:
- Feel free to add some veg! You could try this with finely diced mushroom or peppers.
- Don't overfill the muffin cases – they puff up when they cook. I use small silicone muffin cases. Mine are 5cm / 2in wide at the base.
- If you are cooking for one, halve the ingredients and cook this in the smaller dish.

One Pot

Calories: 406 **Protein:** 35g **Carbs:** 2g **Fat:** 28g

Avocado, Halloumi and Tomato Sourdough Toast

This is one of my favourite ways to start the day – golden sourdough topped with creamy avocado, salty halloumi and juicy roasted tomatoes. It feels like a café brunch, but it only takes 10 minutes. I love it when I want a lighter, veggie-friendly breakfast that still packs in plenty of protein.

SERVES 1

Cook time: 15 minutes

INGREDIENTS:
60g/2oz light halloumi, sliced into 1cm/½in wide strips
small handful of cherry tomatoes, halved
1 large slice of sourdough
½ avocado
juice of ½ lemon
salt and black pepper
basil leaves, to garnish

METHOD:
1. Place the sliced halloumi and cherry tomatoes into the large glass dish of the portable air fryer without the tray. Air fry for 8–10 minutes, flipping the halloumi halfway through the cooking time, until the cheese is golden and the tomatoes have softened.
2. Meanwhile, toast the sourdough slice in a toaster until golden. If you don't have a toaster, you can toast the sourdough in your air fryer for 2 minutes on each side prior to cooking the halloumi and tomatoes.
3. In a small bowl, mash the avocado with most of the lemon juice and some salt and black pepper.
4. Spread the smashed avocado over the toast. Top with the halloumi slices and roasted tomatoes. Finish with an extra squeeze of lemon and a pinch of black pepper, then garnish with the basil and enjoy!

STORE: This recipe is best enjoyed fresh.

MEALS WITH MAX TIPS:
- Add a poached or fried egg on top for extra protein.
- Drizzle with balsamic glaze or honey for a sweet twist. This complements the salty halloumi well!

One Pot

Calories: 488 **Protein:** 26g **Carbs:** 40g **Fat:** 25g

Chicken cooks quickly, making it perfect for when you need to get dinner on the table in a hurry. Most of the recipes here use chicken breast or thighs, but feel free to swap in chicken legs or wings when you have them. Just check the cooking times, as these might take a little longer to cook! Make sure you try out the Harissa Chicken with Chickpeas, Courgette and Crispy Potatoes (page 34) – it's full of colour and flavour and everything cooks together beautifully in one dish.

Harissa Chicken with Chickpeas, Courgette and Crispy Potatoes	34
Sticky Teriyaki Chicken with Broccoli and Noodles	36
Thai-inspired Chicken Satay with Rice	38
Italian Chicken Parmigiana Salad	40
Lemon Garlic Chicken Thighs with Green Beans and Baby Potatoes	42
Mexican Chicken Burrito Bowl	44
Sweet Chilli Chicken Flatbread	46

Chicken

02

Harissa Chicken with Chickpeas, Courgette and Crispy Potatoes

This dish is one of my favourites for a balanced weeknight dinner. The harissa gives the chicken a smoky, spicy kick, while the chickpeas and courgette add freshness and fibre. Crispy potatoes on the side make it feel hearty and satisfying. This colourful dish is the kind of meal that keeps you full for hours.

SERVES 2

Cook time: 35 minutes

INGREDIENTS:
- 200g/7oz Maris Piper potatoes, diced
- 120g/4oz courgette, sliced into half-moons
- 120g/4oz drained tinned chickpeas, rinsed
- 2 tsp olive oil
- 2 tsp garlic granules
- 280g/10oz skinless and boneless chicken thighs
- 2 tbsp harissa paste
- 2 tsp lemon juice, plus extra to serve
- salt and black pepper
- chopped parsley, to garnish

METHOD:
1. In a bowl, mix the diced potatoes, courgette and chickpeas with 1 teaspoon of olive oil, the garlic granules and some salt and black pepper. Add directly to the large glass dish of the portable air fryer, without the tray.
2. Slice the chicken thighs into strips, then place into a bowl with the harissa paste, lemon juice and remaining olive oil. Mix until fully coated.
3. Place the air fryer tray on top of the veg in the dish, and then arrange the chicken on the tray.
4. Air fry for 25–30 minutes until the chicken is golden and the veg is fully cooked. Stir halfway through the cooking time.
5. Divide the crispy potatoes and veg between two plates, then top with the harissa chicken. Squeeze over some lemon juice, garnish with fresh parsley and enjoy. Lovely!

STORE: Cool completely, remove the air fryer tray and seal the glass dish with the lid. Then store in the fridge for up to 3 days.

REHEAT: Remove the lid and attach the portable air fryer. Use the Recrisp function to heat for 7–8 minutes, or until hot throughout. Stir halfway through the cooking time.

PREP AND GO: To prep this ahead of time, follow the above instructions to the end of step 3 and then attach the storage lid. Store in the fridge for up to 3 days. Once ready to cook, attach to the portable air fryer and continue from step 4.

MEALS WITH MAX TIPS:
- Pat the chickpeas dry with kitchen paper before adding. This helps them go golden and crispy in the air fryer.
- Marinate the chicken in the harissa mixture for a few hours (or overnight) for a richer, deeper flavour and juicier chicken.
- If you are cooking for one, halve the ingredients and cook this in the large dish.

Calories: 490　**Protein:** 44g　**Carbs:** 35g　**Fat:** 21g

Sticky Teriyaki Chicken with Broccoli and Noodles

The homemade teriyaki sauce here is sweet and sticky and coats the chicken beautifully. Paired with tender broccoli and noodles, it's a comforting bowl of food that tastes better than a takeaway. I love making this when I'm craving something quick, saucy and satisfying.

SERVES 2

Cook time: 22 minutes

INGREDIENTS:
300g/10½oz chicken breast, cut into bite-sized chunks
140g/5oz broccoli florets, chopped
2 tsp olive oil
2 garlic cloves, finely grated
2 tsp finely grated fresh ginger
200g/7oz egg noodles
salt and black pepper
2 spring onions, thinly sliced, to garnish
2 tsp sesame seeds, to garnish

FOR THE TERIYAKI SAUCE:
2 tbsp soy sauce
2 tbsp honey
2 tsp rice vinegar or white wine vinegar
1 tsp cornflour, mixed with 2 tsp cold water

METHOD:
1. In a bowl, mix the chicken and broccoli with the olive oil, garlic, ginger, salt and black pepper.
2. Add directly to the bottom of the large glass dish of the portable air fryer, without the tray, and spread into an even layer.
3. Air fry for 10 minutes, stirring halfway through the cooking time.
4. While the chicken and broccoli cooks, make the teriyaki sauce. Mix the soy sauce, honey, vinegar and cornflour mixture together in a bowl.
5. Pour the teriyaki sauce over the chicken and broccoli, mix until fully coated and air fry for a further 3–4 minutes.
6. Bring a saucepan of water to the boil, add the noodles and cook for 1–2 minutes.
7. Using tongs, transfer the noodles into the air fryer dish with the broccoli and chicken. Stir until fully combined.
8. Serve in a bowl, garnished with sliced spring onion and sesame seeds. Enjoy!

STORE: Cool the teriyaki chicken and broccoli completely and seal the glass dish with the lid. Then store in the fridge for up to 3 days. Don't cook the noodles at this stage.

REHEAT: Remove the lid and attach the portable air fryer. Use the Recrisp function to heat for 6–7 minutes, or until hot. Cook the noodles a few minutes before it's finished reheating.

PREP AND GO: To prep this ahead of time, follow the above instructions to the end of step 2 and then attach the storage lid. Store in the fridge for up to 2 days. Once ready to cook, attach to the portable air fryer and continue from step 3.

MEALS WITH MAX TIPS:
- Want to mix it up? Feel free to swap the noodles for rice!
- Want it spicy? Add some sliced red chillies to the dish with the chicken and broccoli.
- If you are cooking for one, halve the ingredients and cook this in the smaller dish.

Calories: 496   **Protein:** 43g   **Carbs:** 51g   **Fat:** 14g

Thai-inspired Chicken Satay with Rice

Satay chicken is always a crowd-pleaser, and this lighter version still has all the flavour of the classic. The creamy peanut sauce with lime and chilli makes the chicken irresistible, and serving it with fluffy rice makes it a complete meal. I make this one when I want something vibrant and a little different to my usual midweek dinners.

SERVES 2

Cook time: 20 minutes

INGREDIENTS:
- 300g/10½oz chicken breast, cut into chunks
- 1 tsp olive oil
- 2 tsp curry powder
- 80g/3oz rice
- salt and black pepper
- chopped coriander, to serve
- lime wedges, to serve

FOR THE SATAY SAUCE:
- 4 tsp smooth peanut butter
- 2 tsp soy sauce
- 2 tsp honey
- juice of 1 lime
- 6 tbsp hot water
- 1 tsp chilli flakes

METHOD:
1. Place the chicken into a mixing bowl with the olive oil, curry powder, salt, and black pepper. Mix until the chicken is fully coated.
2. Transfer into the bottom of the large glass dish of the portable air fryer, without the tray, and spread into an even layer.
3. Air fry for 12 minutes, flipping halfway through the cooking time.
4. Cook the rice according to the packet instructions.
5. Meanwhile, in a small jug or bowl, mix all the satay sauce ingredients together.
6. Pour the sauce over the chicken and mix until fully coated.
7. Air fry for a further 3 minutes.
8. Serve with the cooked rice, garnished with chopped fresh coriander and a lime wedge.

STORE: Cool completely and seal the glass dish with the lid. Then store in the fridge for up to 3 days. It's best not to add the sauce until serving, so when reheating, add the sauce during the final 2 minutes.

REHEAT: Remove the lid and attach the portable air fryer. Use the Recrisp function to heat for 7 minutes, or until hot. Mix in the sauce to coat the chicken, then cook on the Recrisp function for a further 2 minutes. Cook your rice according to the packet instructions.

PREP AND GO: To prep this ahead of time, follow the above instructions to the end of step 2 and then attach the storage lid. Keep in the fridge for up to 3 days. You can mix the sauce in advance and store separately, but don't coat the chicken at this stage. When you're ready, continue from step 3.

MEALS WITH MAX TIPS:
- To make prepping this dish even easier, you could swap boiled rice for microwave rice!
- For some freshness and crunch, you could serve this with some shredded carrot, cucumber ribbons and crushed peanuts on the side.
- If you are cooking for one, halve the ingredients and cook this in the smaller dish.

Calories: 473   **Protein:** 41g   **Carbs:** 49g   **Fat:** 12g

Italian Chicken Parmigiana Salad

This recipe takes the classic chicken parmigiana and gives it a lighter twist. You still get that crispy chicken and rich tomato flavour, but it is served over a fresh salad, so it feels much more balanced. It's a great one for summer, or when you want something that feels indulgent without being too heavy.

SERVES 2

Cook time: 15 minutes

INGREDIENTS:
- 2 x 150g/5¼oz chicken breasts
- 2 tbsp plain flour
- 2 eggs
- 8 tbsp panko breadcrumbs
- 2 tbsp grated Parmesan
- 2 tsp dried oregano
- oil spray
- 4 tbsp passata
- 30g/1oz grated light mozzarella
- salt and black pepper
- basil leaves, to garnish

FOR THE SALAD:
- handful of mixed salad leaves
- 10 cherry tomatoes, halved
- 1 red onion, sliced
- 2 tsp balsamic vinegar
- 1 tsp olive oil

METHOD:

1. Carefully slice the chicken breasts in half so you have four thin pieces. Season the chicken with salt and black pepper, then coat in the flour.
2. In one bowl, crack in the eggs and beat with a fork. In another bowl, add the breadcrumbs, Parmesan and dried oregano, and season with salt and black pepper.
3. Coat the chicken in the egg, then in the breadcrumbs. Press in the breadcrumbs to make sure they stick and the chicken is fully coated.
4. Place the coated chicken into the large glass dish of the portable air fryer, on top of the tray.
5. Spray with oil and air fry for 12 minutes, turning halfway through the cooking time, until the chicken is crispy and golden brown.
6. Spoon the passata on top of the chicken and then top with grated mozzarella. Air fry for a further 4 minutes.
7. Meanwhile, make the salad. Place the salad leaves, cherry tomatoes and red onion into a bowl, add the balsamic vinegar and olive oil, and mix until fully coated.
8. Once the chicken is cooked, remove from the air fryer and slice into strips. Serve on top of the salad, garnish with fresh basil, and enjoy.

STORE: Cool the chicken completely and seal the glass dish with the lid. Then store in the fridge for up to 3 days. It's best to make the salad just before serving.

REHEAT: Remove the lid and attach the portable air fryer. Use the Recrisp function to heat for 8 minutes, or until hot. While it reheats, you can prep your salad.

MEALS WITH MAX TIPS:
- Don't have mozzarella? You could mix this up by swapping the mozzarella for feta or Cheddar.
- Dress the salad just before serving. If you dress the salad too early it can become soggy.
- If you are cooking for one, halve the ingredients and cook this in the smaller dish.

One Pot

Calories: 409 **Protein:** 46g **Carbs:** 18g **Fat:** 14g

Lemon Garlic Chicken Thighs with Green Beans and Baby Potatoes

This dish is all about simple, fresh flavours that just work. The chicken thighs are juicy and full of flavour from the lemon and garlic, and pairing them with green beans and baby potatoes makes it a wholesome, no-fuss meal. It's the kind of recipe I come back to again and again.

SERVES 2

Cook time: 25 minutes

INGREDIENTS:
- 4 x 125g/4oz skinless and boneless chicken thighs
- 300g/10½oz baby potatoes, cut into quarters
- 160g/5½oz green beans, trimmed and cut in half
- 4 garlic cloves, finely grated
- grated zest and juice of 2 lemons
- 2 tsp olive oil
- 1 tsp dried thyme
- salt and black pepper
- lemon wedges, to serve

METHOD:
1. In a bowl, add the chicken thighs, baby potatoes, green beans, grated garlic, lemon zest and juice, olive oil, dried thyme, salt and black pepper.
2. Mix until everything is fully coated and then place into the large glass dish of the portable air fryer, on top of the tray. Spread the veg out in a single layer and arrange the chicken thighs on top.
3. Air fry for 20 minutes, stirring halfway through the cooking time (after stirring, make sure the chicken thighs are placed back on top), until the chicken is cooked through.
4. Serve with a lemon wedge on the side and enjoy. Lovely!

STORE: Cool completely and seal the glass dish with the lid. Then store in the fridge for up to 3 days.

REHEAT: Remove the lid and attach the portable air fryer. Use the Recrisp function to heat for 8 minutes, or until hot.

PREP AND GO: To prep this ahead of time, follow the above instructions to the end of step 2 and then attach the storage lid. Store in the fridge for up to 2 days. Once ready to cook, attach to the portable air fryer and continue from step 3.

MEALS WITH MAX TIPS:
- Want it extra crispy? Choose skin-on chicken thighs and cook for an extra 2 minutes at the end. Bear in mind, skin-on chicken thighs are higher in calories.
- Want to mix it up? Swap the green beans for asparagus or courgette.
- If you are cooking for one, halve the ingredients and cook this in the large dish.

One Pot

Calories: 447 **Protein:** 38g **Carbs:** 38g **Fat:** 17g

Mexican Chicken Burrito Bowl

This is my go-to when I want something colourful and packed with flavour. Spiced chicken, rice, salsa and all the toppings – it's a proper build-your-own bowl. I love that you can customise it depending on what you've got in the fridge, and it always feels fresh and filling.

SERVES 2

Cook time: 20 minutes

INGREDIENTS:
- 250g/9oz chicken breast, cut into bite-sized chunks
- 1 red pepper, roughly diced
- 1 red onion, finely diced
- 2 tsp olive oil
- 2 tsp smoked paprika
- 1 tsp ground cumin
- 1 tsp garlic powder
- 1 tsp chilli flakes
- 80g/3oz rice
- 8 cherry tomatoes, cut into quarters
- ½ avocado, diced
- 2 tsp soured cream
- salt and black pepper
- coriander, to garnish
- lime wedges, to serve

METHOD:
1. Add the chicken, pepper, red onion, olive oil, paprika, cumin, garlic powder, chilli flakes, salt and black pepper to a bowl. Mix until fully coated.
2. Place into the large glass dish of the portable air fryer, on top of the tray.
3. Air fry for 15 minutes, stirring halfway through the cooking time.
4. Meanwhile, cook the rice according to the packet instructions.
5. Divide the rice between two serving bowls and top with the chicken and veg, cherry tomatoes and diced avocado. Top each portion with a teaspoon of soured cream, then garnish with fresh coriander and serve with a lime wedge.

STORE: Cool the chicken and veg mixture completely and seal the glass dish with the lid. Then store in the fridge for up to 3 days. It's best to prep the rice, tomatoes and avocado just before serving.

REHEAT: Remove the lid and attach the portable air fryer. Use the Recrisp function to heat for 8 minutes, or until hot. Cook the rice according to the packet instructions.

PREP AND GO: To prep this ahead of time, follow the above instructions to the end of step 2 and then attach the storage lid. Store in the fridge for up to 3 days. Once ready to cook, attach to the portable air fryer and continue from step 3. It's best to prep the tomatoes, avocado and rice while it cooks, rather than in advance.

MEALS WITH MAX TIPS:
- To make the prep easier, you could swap boiled rice for microwave rice.
- You could add some black beans or sweetcorn for extra fibre.
- You could swap the soured cream for 0% fat Greek yogurt to reduce the calories slightly.
- If you are cooking for one, halve the ingredients and cook this in the smaller dish.

Calories: 499 **Protein:** 35g **Carbs:** 55g **Fat:** 15g

PREP + GO

SERVES 2
Cook time: 15 minutes

INGREDIENTS:
2 tsp olive oil
juice of 1 lemon
2 garlic cloves, finely grated
2 tsp dried oregano
2 tsp smoked paprika
300g/10½oz chicken breast, sliced into thin strips
2 tbsp sweet chilli sauce, plus extra to serve
2 flatbreads
½ red onion, thinly sliced
1 tomato, thinly sliced
2 tbsp 0% fat Greek yogurt
salt and black pepper

Sweet Chilli Chicken Flatbread

Sweet chilli chicken is a classic high-protein flavour combination, and serving it on a flatbread makes it quick, fun and a bit different from the usual midweek meal. Portable air fryers like the Ninja Crispi get the chicken perfectly sticky! It really is a lovely dinner – or lunch – that's ready in no time.

METHOD:
1. In a bowl, mix the olive oil, lemon juice, garlic, oregano, paprika, salt and black pepper. Add the chicken and mix until fully coated.
2. Add the chicken in the large glass dish of the portable air fryer on top of the tray.
3. Air fry for 12 minutes, flipping halfway through the cooking time. The chicken should be golden brown and slightly charred at the edges.
4. Add the sweet chilli sauce and mix until the chicken is fully coated. Air fry for an additional 2 minutes.
5. Place the flatbreads on top of the chicken in the air fryer and air fry for 1 minute to warm them.
6. Put the flatbreads on serving plates and spread with the Greek yogurt. Top with the chicken, red onion and tomato. Finish it off with a dollop of Greek yogurt and a drizzle of sweet chilli sauce on top, then wrap the flatbread and enjoy. Lovely!

STORE: Cool the sweet chilli chicken completely and seal the glass dish with the lid. Then store in the fridge for up to 3 days. It's best to assemble the wraps just before serving.

REHEAT: Remove the lid and attach the portable air fryer. Use the Recrisp function to heat for 7–8 minutes, or until hot.

PREP AND GO: To prep this ahead of time, follow the above instructions to the end of step 2 and then attach the storage lid. Store in the fridge for up to 3 days. Once ready to cook, attach to the portable air fryer and continue from step 3.

MEALS WITH MAX TIPS:
- You could mix this up by swapping sweet chilli sauce for BBQ sauce or peri-peri sauce.
- For extra flavour, once you've coated the chicken, you could cover it and leave it in the fridge to marinate for an hour before cooking.
- If you are cooking for one, halve the ingredients and cook this in the smaller dish..

One Pot

Calories: 495   **Protein:** 57g   **Carbs:** 47g   **Fat:** 11g

Beef brings richness and heartiness to any meal, and the portable air fryers like the Ninja Crispi handle it brilliantly. You'll find everything from quick midweek mince dishes to comforting classics. Whether you're after something speedy or a meal that feels extra satisfying, these recipes make the most of beef's deep, savoury flavour – all with minimal effort and maximum taste. If you can handle a bit of spice give the Crispy Chilli Beef with Rice (page 58) a go – it's bold, sticky and every bit as good as your favourite takeaway version.

Beef Kofta Salad with Spiced Chickpeas and Mint Yogurt Sauce	50
Mexican Beef and Black Bean Tacos	52
Greek Beef Meatballs with Courgette, Feta and Lemon Rice	54
Steak Chimichurri Bowl with Crispy Potatoes	56
Crispy Chilli Beef with Rice	58
Beef and Mushroom Stroganoff Traybake	60
Philly Cheesesteak Bake with Peppers and Sweet Potato Wedges	62

Beef

03

Beef Kofta Salad with Spiced Chickpeas and Mint Yogurt Sauce

These koftas are packed with spices. I love pairing them with crispy chickpeas and a cooling mint yogurt – the result is light and fresh, and feels like summer in a bowl. It's also a great one to make ahead for lunches.

SERVES 2

Cook time: 30 minutes

INGREDIENTS:
260g/9oz 12% fat beef mince
2 garlic cloves, finely grated
2 tsp ground cumin
1 tsp ground coriander
big pinch of ground cinnamon
1 tsp olive oil
salt and black pepper
chopped coriander, to garnish

FOR THE CHICKPEAS:
100g/3½oz drained tinned chickpeas, rinsed and patted dry
1 tsp smoked paprika
½ tsp ground cumin
½ tsp garlic powder
1 tsp olive oil

FOR THE MINT YOGURT:
4 tbsp 0% Greek yogurt
2 tsp chopped fresh or dried mint
squeeze of lemon juice

FOR THE SALAD:
handful of mixed salad leaves
½ cucumber, diced
80g/3oz cherry tomatoes, halved
1 red onion, thinly sliced
2 tsp olive oil
squeeze of lemon juice

METHOD:
1. In a bowl, mix the beef, garlic, cumin, coriander, cinnamon, salt and black pepper. Shape into 4–6 small oval koftas (sausage shapes). Set aside.
2. In the large glass dish of the portable air fryer, without the tray, toss the chickpeas with the spices, olive oil and a pinch of salt. Put the tray on top above the chickpeas, lightly coat the koftas with olive oil, then place the koftas onto the tray.
3. Air fry the beef and the chickpeas for 15–20 minutes, turning halfway through the cooking time.
4. Meanwhile, for the mint yogurt, mix the Greek yogurt, mint, lemon juice and a pinch of salt in a small bowl. Set aside.
5. Make the salad by tossing the salad leaves, cucumber, tomatoes and onion with the olive oil, lemon juice, salt and pepper.
6. Divide the salad between two bowls and top with the koftas and crispy chickpeas. Drizzle the mint yogurt over the top and garnish with fresh coriander.

STORE: Cool completely and seal the glass dish with the lid. It's best to store the salad and sauce separately. The koftas and chickpeas can be stored together. Keep in the fridge for up to 3 days.

REHEAT: Remove the lid and attach the portable air fryer. Use the Recrisp function to heat the koftas and chickpeas for 8 minutes, or until hot, stirring halfway through.

PREP AND GO: To prep this ahead of time, follow the above instructions to the end of step 2 and then attach the storage lid. Prep the mint yogurt sauce and store separately. You can prep your salad in advance, but don't cover in the dressing until you're ready to serve. Place everything into the fridge for up to 3 days. Once ready to cook, attach to the portable air fryer and continue from step 3, prepping the salad and dressing while the beef cooks, if not already prepped.

MEALS WITH MAX TIPS:
- When mixing the kofta mixture, combine everything until it just holds, rather than overworking the mince. Overmixing can make them tough.
- If you can, use fresh mint for the yogurt sauce, as the flavour is much more vibrant.
- Make sure you dry the chickpeas well before air frying, as they will get crispier.
- If you are cooking for one, halve the ingredients and cook this in the smaller dish.

One Pot

Calories: 446   **Protein:** 44g   **Carbs:** 19g   **Fat:** 23g

SERVES 2
Cook time: 20 minutes

INGREDIENTS:
200g/7oz 12% fat beef mince
70g/2½oz drained tinned black beans, rinsed
2 tsp tomato purée
2 tsp olive oil
1 tsp smoked paprika
½ tsp ground cumin
1 tsp garlic granules
big pinch of chilli flakes
4 small tortillas
4 tsp soured cream
½ red onion, finely diced
20g/¾oz Cheddar, grated
salt and black pepper
chopped coriander, to garnish
lime wedges, to serve

Mexican Beef and Black Bean Tacos

Tacos are always a winner, and this recipe is one of my favourites. The beef is seasoned with Mexican spices and combined with black beans for extra protein and fibre. Pile them high with salsa, soured cream or whatever toppings you like – they're quick, fun and perfect for a weeknight.

METHOD:
1. Add the beef mince, drained black beans, tomato purée, olive oil and the dry seasonings directly to the large glass dish of the portable air fryer, without the tray.
2. Mix well until fully combined.
3. Air fry for 15 minutes, stirring and breaking it up every 5 minutes, until the beef is fully cooked and the mixture is thick.
4. Arrange the tortillas flat on plates and divide the beef mixture among them.
5. Top each taco with a teaspoon of soured cream, some diced red onion and some grated cheese. Garnish with chopped fresh coriander.
6. Serve with lime wedges for squeezing over and then enjoy. Lovely!

STORE: Cool the beef mixture completely and seal the glass dish with the lid. Then store in the fridge for up to 2 days. Store the tortillas and toppings separately.

REHEAT: Remove the lid and attach the portable air fryer. Add a splash of water to loosen it a little. Use the Recrisp function to heat for 8 minutes until hot, stirring halfway through.

PREP AND GO: The beef mixture can be made in advance and cooked when needed. Follow the above instructions to the end of step 2 and then attach the storage lid. Keep chilled in the fridge for up to 24 hours. Complete the remaining steps when you're ready to eat.

MEALS WITH MAX TIPS:
- You can also make these with chicken. Swap the minced beef for diced chicken breast.
- If you are cooking for one, halve the ingredients and cook this in the smaller dish.

One Pot

Calories: 479   **Protein:** 31g   **Carbs:** 40g   **Fat:** 22g

Greek Beef Meatballs with Courgette, Feta and Lemon Rice

These Greek-inspired meatballs are packed with flavour, and pair beautifully with the lemony rice and feta. The courgette adds freshness, and the air fryer gets the meatballs golden on the outside while keeping them tender inside. It's a bright, balanced dish I love making when I want something filling but not heavy.

SERVES 2

Cook time: 25 minutes

INGREDIENTS:
250g/9oz 12% fat beef mince
½ red onion, finely diced
2 garlic cloves, grated
1 tsp dried oregano
1 tsp ground cumin
grated zest of ½ lemon and juice of 1 lemon
1 small courgette, roughly chopped
oil spray
80g/3oz rice
2 tbsp Greek yogurt
50g/1¾oz feta, crumbled
salt and black pepper
chopped parsley, to garnish

METHOD:
1. In a bowl, mix the beef mince, red onion, garlic, oregano, cumin, lemon zest, salt and black pepper. Shape into 6–8 small meatballs.
2. Place the tray into the large glass dish of the portable air fryer and arrange the meatballs on the tray, placing them in the middle.
3. Add the chopped courgette around the outside of the meatballs, then season the courgette with salt and black pepper.
4. Spray the meatballs and courgette with a little oil, then air fry for 15 minutes, turning halfway through the cooking time.
5. Before the meatballs and courgette have finished cooking, cook the rice according to the packet instructions.
6. Once the rice is ready, pour it into a bowl and squeeze in the lemon juice. Mix until all the rice is coated.
7. Divide the rice between two plates, then top with the meatballs and the courgette. Add a tablespoon of Greek yogurt to each portion, crumble over the feta and garnish with chopped fresh parsley.

STORE: Cool the meatballs and courgettes completely and seal the glass dish with the lid. Store in the fridge for up to 2 days. Cook the rice and add the feta when you're ready to eat.

REHEAT: Remove the lid and attach the portable air fryer. Use the Recrisp function to heat for 6–7 minutes until hot. Heat the rice in the microwave while the meatballs and courgette are reheating.

MEALS WITH MAX TIPS:
- Want to switch it up? Try using turkey or pork mince instead of beef.
- Want to turn up the heat? Sprinkle over some chilli flakes when plating up!
- If you are cooking for one, halve the ingredients and cook this in the large dish.
- You can use microwave rice to save time, if you want.

Calories: 493   **Protein:** 35g   **Carbs:** 36g   **Fat:** 25g

Steak Chimichurri Bowl with Crispy Potatoes

This is such a bold, vibrant dish. The steak is juicy and flavourful, but it's the fresh chimichurri that really makes it special. Served with crispy potatoes and salad, it's hearty and refreshing at the same time. I make this when I want something that feels restaurant-quality at home.

SERVES 2

Cook time: 25 minutes

INGREDIENTS:
300g/10½oz baby potatoes, diced small
4 tsp olive oil
300g/10½oz sirloin steak
2 tsp red wine vinegar
handful of parsley, finely chopped
1 garlic clove, finely chopped
1 tsp dried oregano
½ red chilli, finely chopped
grated zest and juice of 1 lemon
salt and black pepper
salad leaves, to serve

METHOD:
1. Add the diced potatoes, 2 teaspoons of the olive oil and a pinch of salt and pepper to the large glass dish of the portable air fryer, without the tray. Mix well until the potatoes are evenly coated.
2. Air fry for 18 minutes, stirring halfway through the cooking time, until golden and crispy.
3. Meanwhile, season the steak with salt and pepper. Let it sit at room temperature for 10 minutes.
4. In a small bowl, mix the vinegar, chopped parsley, garlic, oregano, red chilli, lemon zest and juice and remaining 2 teaspoons of olive oil to make the chimichurri.
5. Once the potatoes are almost done, place the tray on top, and arrange the steak on the tray. Air fry for 6 minutes, flipping halfway through the cooking time, or until cooked to your liking.
6. Rest the steak for 2 minutes, then slice.
7. Serve the sliced steak over the potatoes, spoon over the chimichurri sauce and serve with some salad leaves on the side.

STORE: It's best to cook the steak on the day you plan to eat it, otherwise it can become tough when reheated!

MEALS WITH MAX TIPS:
- Don't skip the resting time, it keeps the steak juicy and flavourful.
- You could swap the steak for halloumi or portobello mushrooms for a veggie version, or have them as an extra!
- If you are cooking for one, halve the ingredients and cook this in the smaller dish.

One Pot

Calories: 451   **Protein:** 30g   **Carbs:** 26g   **Fat:** 26g

 PREP + GO

Crispy Chilli Beef with Rice

This classic is one of my absolute favourites to make at home. The beef goes beautifully crispy in the portable air fryer and the sticky chilli sauce coats every piece. Served with rice, it's sweet, spicy and unbelievably moreish – and so much lighter than the takeaway version.

SERVES 2

Cook time: 20 minutes

INGREDIENTS:
- 220g/8oz sirloin steak, thinly sliced
- 2 tsp cornflour
- 2 tsp light soy sauce
- 1 tsp sesame oil
- 2 tsp olive oil
- 1 red pepper, thinly sliced
- 2 garlic cloves, finely chopped
- 1 tsp grated fresh ginger
- 2 tbsp sweet chilli sauce
- 2 tsp dark soy sauce
- juice of 1 lime
- big pinch of chilli flakes
- 80g/3oz rice
- 2 spring onions, sliced
- chopped coriander, to garnish

METHOD:
1. In a bowl, toss the sliced beef with the cornflour, light soy sauce and sesame oil. Let it marinate while you prep everything else.
2. Add the olive oil, red pepper, garlic and ginger to the large glass dish of the portable air fryer, without the tray. Air fry for 5 minutes.
3. Place the tray on top of the peppers, then arrange the marinated beef on top.
4. Air fry for 10–12 minutes, stirring halfway through the cooking time, until the beef is crispy and cooked through.
5. Remove the tray and add the beef to the bottom of the dish with the peppers.
6. Stir in the sweet chilli sauce, dark soy sauce, lime juice and chilli flakes. Mix until everything is fully coated.
7. Air fry for 2 minutes until sticky and glossy.
8. Meanwhile, cook the rice according to the packet instructions.
9. Divide the cooked rice between two plates and top with the crispy chilli beef and the sliced spring onions. Garnish with fresh coriander, then enjoy.

STORE: Cool the crispy chilli beef completely and seal the glass dish with the lid. It's best to cook the rice while reheating the crispy chilli beef and add the spring onions when serving.

REHEAT: Remove the lid and attach the portable air fryer. Use the Recrisp function to heat the crispy chilli beef for 6–7 minutes. Cook the rice while it reheats.

MEALS WITH MAX TIPS:
- Want to bulk it out? Add some cooked broccoli or green beans.
- You can swap the steak for thin strips of chicken or tofu, if you like.
- If you are cooking for one, halve the ingredients and cook this in the smaller dish.
- To make prepping this dish even easier, you could swap boiled rice for microwave rice!

Calories: 497 **Protein:** 30g **Carbs:** 42g **Fat:** 25g

Beef and Mushroom Stroganoff Traybake

This dish is pure comfort food. The beef and mushrooms cook together in a creamy sauce, and baking it all in one dish makes it so easy. It's rich but still lighter than the traditional version.

SERVES 2

Cook time: 25 minutes

INGREDIENTS:
- 2 tsp olive oil
- 1 red onion, thinly sliced
- 150g/5¼oz chestnut mushrooms, sliced
- 2 garlic cloves, grated
- 250g/9oz rump steak, sliced into strips
- 1 tsp smoked paprika
- 2 tsp Worcestershire sauce
- 2 tsp Dijon mustard
- 130g/4½oz tagliatelle, or your preferred pasta shape
- 120ml/4fl oz beef stock
- 2 tbsp low-fat crème fraîche
- salt and black pepper
- finely chopped parsley, to garnish

METHOD:
1. Add the olive oil, onion, mushrooms and garlic to the large glass dish of the portable air fryer, without the tray.
2. Air fry for 6 minutes until softened.
3. Add the beef strips, smoked paprika, Worcestershire sauce, mustard and a pinch of salt and pepper. Mix well so everything is fully coated.
4. Air fry for 10 minutes, stirring halfway through the cooking time, until the beef is cooked and lightly browned.
5. Meanwhile, cook the pasta according to the packet instructions.
6. Add the beef stock to the stroganoff and stir through. Air fry for 2 minutes to reduce slightly.
7. Remove from the air fryer and stir in the crème fraîche until creamy.
8. Serve the stroganoff over the cooked pasta and garnish with fresh parsley. Lovely!

STORE: Cool completely and seal the glass dish with the lid. If cooking in advance, don't cook the pasta or add the crème fraîche, as it can split when reheated.

REHEAT: Remove the lid and attach the portable air fryer. Use the Recrisp function and cook for 7 minutes, then stir through the crème fraiche. Cook the pasta while it reheats.

MEALS WITH MAX TIPS:
- Stroganoff too runny? Air fry for an extra 2 minutes to thicken the sauce.
- Want extra nutrients? Add some spinach during the final 2 minutes of cooking.
- If you are cooking for one, halve the ingredients and cook this in the smaller dish.

Calories: 498   **Protein:** 39g   **Carbs:** 58g   **Fat:** 13g

Philly Cheesesteak Bake with Peppers and Sweet Potato Wedges

This recipe is inspired by the classic Philly cheesesteak sandwich. Tender strips of beef, gooey melted cheese and sweet peppers are all baked together, then served with crispy sweet potato wedges on the side. It's hearty, indulgent and perfect for when you're craving comfort food.

SERVES 2

Cook time: 25 minutes

INGREDIENTS:
- 400g/14oz sweet potato, cut into thin wedges
- 2 tsp smoked paprika
- 2 tsp garlic granules
- 2 tsp olive oil
- 300g/10½oz rump steak, thinly sliced
- 1 red pepper, sliced
- 1 green pepper, sliced
- ½ red onion, sliced
- 50g/1¾oz light Cheddar or mozzarella, grated
- salt and black pepper

METHOD:
1. Add the sweet potato wedges, paprika, garlic granules, a pinch of salt and pepper and 1 teaspoon of the olive oil to the large glass dish of the portable air fryer, without the tray. Mix until fully coated.
2. Air fry for 10 minutes, flipping halfway through the cooking time.
3. Meanwhile, in a bowl, toss the beef strips with the remaining oil and a pinch of salt and pepper.
4. After 10 minutes, place the air fryer tray on top of the sweet potato wedges. Add the beef, peppers and onion to the tray.
5. Air fry for 8 minutes, stirring halfway through the cooking time, until the beef is cooked and the veg has softened.
6. Sprinkle the grated cheese evenly over the beef and veg.
7. Air fry for 2–3 minutes until melted and bubbling.
8. Serve the sweet potato wedges topped with the cheesy veg and steak.

STORE: Cool completely and seal the glass dish with the lid. If cooking in advance, don't add the cheese.

REHEAT: Remove the lid and attach the portable air fryer. Use the Recrisp function and cook for 7 minutes, then add the cheese and cook for 1–2 more minutes.

PREP AND GO: Prep the wedges as in step 1, then attach the lid. Prep the onions, peppers and steak and store separately in the fridge for up to 24 hours. Cook following the instructions from step 2 when you're ready to eat.

MEALS WITH MAX TIPS:
- For extra cheesiness, add a second cheese like a light cream cheese. Stir this through before topping with the grated cheese.
- Want more volume? Throw in sliced mushrooms or courgette with the peppers.
- If you are cooking for one, halve the ingredients and cook this in the smaller dish.

One Pot

Calories: 489 **Protein:** 44g **Carbs:** 40g **Fat:** 17g

Pork is full of flavour and crisps up beautifully in the air fryer. From tenderloin to juicy chops, these recipes show how versatile this meat can be. Pat your pork dry before cooking – it helps the edges caramelise for that perfect golden crust. Whether you like it sticky, spicy, or smoky, you'll find something here to make any night feel like a treat. For a recipe bursting with fresh Mediterranean flavours, check out the tender and garlicky Greek Pork Gyros with Tzatziki (page 68).

Italian Style Pork and Fennel Meatballs with Spaghetti	66
Greek Pork Gyros with Tzatziki	68
Sausage and Veg Traybake with a Sticky Maple Glaze	70
BBQ Pork Tacos with Coleslaw	72
Garlic and Rosemary Pork Chops with Baby Potatoes	74
Pesto Pork with Courgette and Cherry Tomatoes	76
Miso Pork with Sesame Broccoli and Rice	78

Pork

04

Italian Style Pork and Fennel Meatballs with Spaghetti

These meatballs are a real comfort classic. The pork and fennel give them a lovely flavour, and they cook up beautifully golden in the portable air fryer. Tossed with spaghetti and a rich tomato sauce, it's a dish that feels cosy and satisfying, without being too heavy.

SERVES 2

Cook time: 25 minutes

INGREDIENTS:
260g/9 ½ oz 5% fat pork mince
1 tsp dried fennel seeds, crushed
2 tsp garlic granules
2 tsp dried oregano
2 tsp olive oil
350ml/12fl oz passata
2 tsp tomato purée
2 garlic cloves, finely grated
small handful of basil leaves, plus extra to garnish
120g/4oz dried spaghetti
salt and black pepper
finely grated Parmesan, to serve

METHOD:
1. In a bowl, mix pork mince with the crushed fennel, garlic granules, oregano, salt and black pepper.
2. Shape into 8 small meatballs. Lightly oil the meatballs with the olive oil, then place onto the tray in the large glass dish of the portable air fryer. Air fry for 10 minutes, turning halfway through the cooking time.
3. Boil the spaghetti in salted water until al dente (cooked but still slightly firm), then drain the spaghetti and set aside.
4. In a mixing bowl, combine the passata, tomato purée, garlic, a splash of water, salt and black pepper.
5. Once the meatballs are browned, remove the tray and transfer the meatballs directly into the bottom of the dish. Pour the sauce over them and tear in a few fresh basil leaves. Mix to coat the meatballs. Return to the air fryer and cook for 8 minutes, stirring halfway through the cooking time.
6. Once the meatballs have cooked, add the pasta and mix to coat the spaghetti in the sauce.
7. Serve topped with grated Parmesan and a few fresh basil leaves to garnish. Lovely!

STORE: Cool completely and seal the glass dish with the lid, then store in the fridge for up to 3 days. It's best to store the pasta separately (it soaks up the sauce) but not essential.

REHEAT: Remove the lid and attach the portable air fryer. Add a splash of water to loosen the sauce. Use the Recrisp function to heat for 8 minutes, or until hot, stirring halfway through.

MEALS WITH MAX TIPS:
- Add a pinch of chilli flakes to the sauce for more depth and heat.
- Mix and form the pork mince into meatballs gently to ensure they stay soft and moist. Overworking the mince can make them tougher.
- If you are cooking for one, halve the ingredients and cook this in the smaller dish.

One Pot

Calories: 491   **Protein:** 42g   **Carbs:** 47g   **Fat:** 15g

Greek Pork Gyros with Tzatziki

This recipe takes inspiration from the Greek classic – juicy pork cooked with herbs and spices, served up in flatbreads with cooling tzatziki. It's colourful, fresh and perfect for a fun weekend dinner where everyone can build their own wraps.

SERVES 2
Cook time: 22 minutes

INGREDIENTS:
- 360g/12½oz pork loin, sliced into thin strips
- 2 tsp olive oil
- juice of 1 lemon
- 2 garlic cloves, finely grated
- 1 tsp dried oregano
- big pinch of ground cumin
- 2 flatbreads
- 1 tomato, sliced
- ½ red onion, sliced
- salt and black pepper

FOR THE TZATZIKI:
- 6 tbsp 0% fat Greek yogurt
- ½ small cucumber, grated and squeezed dry
- 1 garlic clove, finely grated
- 2 tsp white wine vinegar or lemon juice
- 2 tsp dried or chopped fresh dill

METHOD:
1. In a bowl, toss the sliced pork with the olive oil, lemon juice, garlic, oregano, cumin, salt and pepper.
2. Place the marinated pork pieces into the large glass dish of the portable air fryer on top of the tray.
3. Air fry for 14–16 minutes, stirring once halfway through the cooking time, until golden, juicy and cooked through.
4. Meanwhile, make the tzatziki by combining the yogurt, grated cucumber, garlic, vinegar or lemon juice, dill and a pinch of salt. Mix until fully combined, then chill in the fridge.
5. Warm the flatbreads in the air fryer or oven for 1–2 minutes.
6. Spread some tzatziki on the flatbreads, then top with the pork, sliced tomato, red onion and the remaining tzatziki. Serve and enjoy!

STORE: Cool the gyros completely and seal the glass dish with the lid. Store in the fridge for up to 3 days. Store the tzatziki separately. Warm the flatbreads and prep the salad when serving.

REHEAT: Remove the lid and attach the portable air fryer. Use the Recrisp function and cook for 7 minutes, then build your gyros following the instructions above.

PREP AND GO: Prep the pork up to the end of step 2, cover the dish with a lid and store in the fridge for up to 24 hours. Once ready to cook, attach to the portable air fryer and continue from step 3. You can prep the tzatziki in advance and store this separately in the fridge, too.

MEALS WITH MAX TIPS:
- Fancy a low-carb option? Swap the flatbread for salad.
- Add a pinch of smoked paprika and chilli flakes to the pork marinade for a smoky, spicy twist.
- If you are cooking for one, halve the ingredients and cook this in the smaller dish.

Calories: 493   **Protein:** 53g   **Carbs:** 45g   **Fat:** 14g

Sausage and Veg Traybake with a Sticky Maple Glaze

Traybakes are always a lifesaver on busy days, and this one couldn't be easier. Juicy sausages are roasted with colourful vegetables and coated in a sweet maple glaze – everything cooks together so the flavours mingle beautifully. It's simple, hearty and full of goodness.

SERVES 2

Cook time: 25 minutes

INGREDIENTS:
250g/9oz baby potatoes, cut into quarters
1 carrot, sliced into batons
1 red pepper, cut into chunks
1 red onion, cut into wedges
2 tsp olive oil
4 pork sausages
salt and black pepper

FOR THE STICKY MUSTARD GLAZE:
2 tbsp honey
2 tsp wholegrain mustard
2 tsp Dijon mustard
2 tsp balsamic vinegar

METHOD:
1. In a bowl, mix the potatoes, carrot, pepper and onion with the olive oil, salt and pepper.
2. Add the vegetables directly to the bottom of the large glass dish of the portable air fryer without the tray, spreading them out evenly.
3. Place the sausages on top of the vegetables in the middle.
4. Air fry for 12 minutes, mixing once halfway through the cooking time. After mixing, make sure the sausages are placed back on the top of the veg.
5. Meanwhile, make the glaze by combining the honey, wholegrain mustard, Dijon mustard and balsamic vinegar in a small bowl.
6. After 12 minutes, drizzle the glaze over the sausages and vegetables, mix gently and air fry for a further 8 minutes until the sausages are cooked through and the vegetables are tender.
7. Serve hot, spooning any excess glaze from the dish over the top.

STORE: Cool completely and seal the glass dish with the lid. Then store in the fridge for up to 3 days.

REHEAT: Remove the lid and attach the portable air fryer. Use the Recrisp function to heat for 7–8 minutes, or until hot, stirring halfway through.

PREP AND GO: Prep up to step 3, cover the dish with a lid and store in the fridge for up to 24 hours. You can prep the glaze in advance and store this separately in the fridge, too. Once ready to cook, attach to the portable air fryer and continue from step 4.

MEALS WITH MAX TIPS:
- Swap the pork sausages for chicken or veggie sausages for a lighter option.
- Add extra vegetables like courgette or cherry tomatoes for more colour and nutrients. Or some sliced chilli for heat!
- If you are cooking for one, halve the ingredients and cook this in the large dish.

One Pot

- **Calories:** 468
- **Protein:** 18g
- **Carbs:** 55g
- **Fat:** 21g

PREP + GO

SERVES 2
Cook time: 20 minutes

INGREDIENTS:
320g/11½oz pork fillet, sliced into thin strips
1 tsp olive oil
1 tsp smoked paprika
1 tsp garlic powder
1 tsp onion powder
8 tsp BBQ sauce
4 small soft tortillas
salt and black pepper
chopped coriander, to garnish

FOR THE COLESLAW:
80g/3oz white cabbage, finely shredded
60g/2oz carrot, grated
2 tbsp light mayonnaise
2 tsp apple cider vinegar
salt and black pepper

BBQ Pork Tacos with Coleslaw

Pork and BBQ sauce are a match made in heaven, and they taste even better stuffed into tacos. The portable air fryer makes the pork tender and sticky, and the crunchy coleslaw adds freshness. It's messy, fun and exactly what you want from taco night.

METHOD:
1. In a bowl, mix the pork strips with the olive oil, smoked paprika, garlic powder, onion powder, salt and black pepper.
2. Place into the large glass dish of the portable air fryer, without the tray, spreading it out evenly.
3. Air fry for 10 minutes, stirring halfway through the cooking time, until cooked through and juicy.
4. Meanwhile, make the coleslaw by combining the cabbage, carrot, mayonnaise, vinegar, salt and black pepper in a bowl. Mix well and chill in the fridge.
5. Add the BBQ sauce to the cooked pork, stir until the pork is fully coated, then return to the portable air fryer for 1–2 minutes to glaze.
6. Warm the tortillas in the portable air fryer for the final minute of cooking.
7. Fill each tortilla with BBQ pork, top with coleslaw and garnish with chopped coriander.

STORE: Cool the pork completely and seal the glass dish with the lid. Then store in the fridge for up to 3 days. Store the coleslaw separately in a sealed container, then build the tacos when you're ready to eat.

REHEAT: Remove the lid and attach the portable air fryer. Use the Recrisp function to heat for 6 minutes, or until hot, stirring halfway through.

PREP AND GO: Prep the pork to step 2, then store in the fridge for up to 24 hours. Once ready to cook, attach to the portable air fryer and continue from step 3. Make the coleslaw ahead and store separately in a sealed container in the fridge.

MEALS WITH MAX TIPS:
- For extra heat, add sliced jalapeños or a pinch of chilli flakes to the pork before cooking.
- Swap tortillas for lettuce cups or a salad for a lighter, lower-carb and lower-calorie option.
- If you are cooking for one, halve the ingredients and cook this in the smaller dish..

One Pot

● **Calories:** 488   ● **Protein:** 38g   ● **Carbs:** 48g   ● **Fat:** 16g

PREP + GO

Garlic and Rosemary Pork Chops with Baby Potatoes

This is a proper classic dinner. Pork chops and baby potatoes infused with garlic and rosemary, – it's simple but packed with flavour. Cooking the chops in the portable air fryer keeps them juicy with golden edges, and the whole plate feels like comfort food done right.

SERVES 2
Cook time: 25 minutes

INGREDIENTS:
- 2 tsp olive oil
- 2 garlic cloves, grated
- 1 tsp dried rosemary
- 2 boneless pork chops, trimmed of excess fat
- 300g/10½oz baby potatoes, halved
- 160g/5½oz broccoli, trimmed
- salt and black pepper

METHOD:
1. In a bowl, mix the olive oil, garlic, rosemary and a big pinch of salt and black pepper. Rub half the mixture over the pork chops.
2. Toss the baby potatoes in the remaining garlic-rosemary oil.
3. Place the potatoes in the large glass dish of the portable air fryer, without the tray.
4. Air fry for 8 minutes, stirring halfway through the cooking time.
5. Push the potatoes to one side of the dish, then add the pork chop to the other side, with the broccoli next to them.
6. Air fry for a further 14 minutes, turning the chops halfway through the cooking time, until the potatoes are starting to crisp, the broccoli is tender and the pork is cooked through.
7. Rest the pork chops for 2 minutes before serving with the potatoes and broccoli. Spoon any remaining garlic-rosemary oil from the dish over the pork chops, then enjoy. Lovely!

STORE: Cool completely and seal the glass dish with the lid. Then store in the fridge for up to 3 days.

REHEAT: Remove the lid and attach the portable air fryer. Use the Recrisp function to heat for 7 minutes, or until hot, stirring halfway through.

PREP AND GO: Prep to step 3, cover with the lid, and store in the fridge for up to 24 hours. Once ready to cook, attach to the portable air fryer and continue from step 4.

MEALS WITH MAX TIPS:
- Swap the pork for chicken breast or salmon fillet, adjusting the cooking times as needed.
- Add lemon zest to the garlic-rosemary oil for a fresh citrusy twist.
- If you are cooking for one, halve the ingredients and cook this in the large dish.

One Pot

● **Calories:** 450   ● **Protein:** 41g   ● **Carbs:** 32g   ● **Fat:** 17g

Pesto Pork with Courgette and Cherry Tomatoes

Pesto makes everything better, and here it transforms pork into a vibrant, Mediterranean-style dish. The courgette and cherry tomatoes add freshness and colour, while the portable air fryer does all the hard work. It's light, fragrant and a lovely change from heavier dinners.

SERVES 2

Cook time: 20 minutes

INGREDIENTS:
- 400g/14oz pork tenderloin, cut into bite-sized pieces
- 2 tsp olive oil
- 300g/10½oz courgette, sliced into half-moons
- 200g/7oz cherry tomatoes, halved
- 3 tbsp green pesto
- 50g/1¾oz feta
- salt and black pepper

METHOD:
1. In a bowl, mix the pork pieces with the olive oil and a good pinch of salt and black pepper.
2. Place the pork and courgette into the large glass dish of the portable air fryer, without the tray.
3. Air fry for 8 minutes, stirring halfway through the cooking time.
4. Add the cherry tomatoes and pesto, stir well and air fry for a further 7 minutes until the pork is cooked through and the vegetables are tender.
5. Serve the pork, courgette and cherry tomatoes on plates or in bowls, spooning over any pesto juices from the dish. Crumble over the feta, then enjoy.

STORE: Cool completely and seal the glass dish with the lid. Then store in the fridge for up to 3 days. Don't add the feta until ready to serve.

REHEAT: Remove the lid and attach the portable air fryer. Use the Recrisp function to heat for 5–6 minutes, or until hot, stirring halfway through, then crumble over the feta.

PREP AND GO: Prep to the end of step 2, cover with the lid and store in the fridge for up to 24 hours. Once ready to cook, attach to the portable air fryer and continue from step 3.

MEALS WITH MAX TIPS:
- Try swapping green pesto for red pesto for a richer, sun-dried tomato flavour.
- Serve with pasta, rice or crusty bread for a more filling meal.
- If you are cooking for one, halve the ingredients and cook this in the large dish.

One Pot

Calories: 464   **Protein:** 50g   **Carbs:** 10g   **Fat:** 24g

Miso Pork with Sesame Broccoli and Rice

PREP + GO

SERVES 2

Cook time: 22 minutes

This dish is packed with umami from the miso, giving the pork a deep, savoury flavour. Paired with sesame broccoli and rice, it's a balanced meal that's both nourishing and comforting. I love making this one when I'm craving something full of flavour.

INGREDIENTS:
- 1 tsp olive oil
- 2 tbsp white miso paste
- 2 tbsp light soy sauce
- 2 tsp honey
- 2 tsp rice vinegar
- 2 garlic cloves, grated
- 2 tsp grated fresh ginger
- 340g/12oz pork tenderloin, sliced into thin strips
- 200g/7oz Tenderstem broccoli
- 1 tsp sesame oil
- 80g/3oz rice
- 2 tsp toasted sesame seeds

METHOD:
1. In a bowl, whisk together the olive oil, miso paste, soy sauce, honey, rice vinegar, garlic and ginger.
2. Add the sliced pork strips to the bowl, toss to coat and let it marinate for at least 5 minutes (or overnight if prepping ahead).
3. Place the pork and any excess marinade on top of the tray in the large glass dish of the portable air fryer.
4. Air fry for 6 minutes, stirring halfway through the cooking time.
5. Add the broccoli, drizzle with sesame oil and air fry for a further 10 minutes, stirring halfway through the cooking time. The pork should be cooked through, and the broccoli should be tender and slightly crisp.
6. Meanwhile, cook the rice according to the packet instructions.
7. Serve the miso pork and sesame broccoli over the rice, and sprinkle the toasted sesame seeds on top. Lovely!

STORE: Cool completely and seal the glass dish with the lid. Then store in the fridge for up to 3 days. Cook the rice when ready to serve.

REHEAT: Remove the lid and attach the portable air fryer. Use the Recrisp function to heat for 6 minutes, or until hot, stirring halfway through. Cook the rice separately before serving.

PREP AND GO: You can marinate the pork in the miso mixture up to 24 hours in advance. Prep to step 3, attach the lid and store in the fridge. The broccoli can be washed, trimmed and stored in the fridge ready to cook. Once ready to cook, attach to the portable air fryer and continue from step 4.

MEALS WITH MAX TIPS:
- You could add some sliced red chilli for a spicy kick.
- To switch up the carb source, you can swap the jasmine rice for brown rice or noodles.
- If you are cooking for one, halve the ingredients and cook this in the large dish.
- You can use microwave rice to save time, if you want.

Calories: 496   **Protein:** 44g   **Carbs:** 43g   **Fat:** 15g

Cooking fish in the air fryer keeps it tender on the inside and crisp on the outside – no soggy edges, no greasy pans. From fillets to fishcakes, these recipes make seafood effortless. Thinner fillets cook fast, so keep an eye on them to avoid overcooking. A squeeze of lemon or a spoonful of sauce is all you need to finish things off. I particularly love the Thai Green Cod Traybake (page 82) – fresh, fragrant and full of punchy flavours that all come together beautifully in one dish.

Thai Green Cod Traybake	82
Italian Tuna Melt Pasta Bake	84
Cajun Cod with Spinach, Roasted Peppers and Turmeric Rice	86
Prawn Tacos with Mango Salsa and Lime Yogurt	88
Crispy Salmon Fishcakes with Cucumber Salad and Mint Yogurt	90
Smoky Paprika Prawn Salad Bowl	92
Chilli Lemon Salmon with Corn Salsa and Zesty Rice	94

Fish

05

Thai Green Cod Traybake

This traybake is bursting with Thai-inspired flavour from the fragrant green curry paste. The cod stays tender while the vegetables soak up all that spicy, creamy sauce. It's an easy, one-dish dinner that feels vibrant and exciting without any fuss.

SERVES 2

Cook time: 30 minutes

INGREDIENTS:
- 1 tbsp coconut oil
- 300g/10½oz baby new potatoes, halved
- 1 red pepper, sliced into strips
- 1 courgette, sliced into half-moons
- 2 x 200g/7oz cod fillets
- salt and black pepper
- coriander leaves, to garnish
- lime wedges, to serve

FOR THE THAI GREEN SAUCE:
- 4 tsp Thai green curry paste
- 100ml/3½fl oz light coconut milk
- 2 tsp fish sauce
- juice of ½ lime

METHOD:
1. Add the coconut oil, potatoes, red pepper and courgette to the large glass dish. Season with salt and black pepper.
2. Air fry for 1 minute until the coconut oil is melted and then stir until the veg is coated in oil.
3. Cook on the Roast for setting 13–15 minutes.
4. Meanwhile, mix all the Thai green sauce ingredients in a small bowl. Set aside.
5. Stir the vegetables, then nestle the cod fillets in the middle of the dish. Pour the sauce evenly over the fish and veg.
6. Roast for a further 8–10 minutes, or until the cod flakes easily and the potatoes are tender.
7. Garnish with coriander and serve with lime wedges. Lovely!

STORE: Best eaten fresh. But if you plan to eat later, cool completely and seal the glass dish with the lid. Then store in the fridge for up to 1 day.

REHEAT: Remove the lid and attach the portable air fryer. Use the Recrisp function to heat for 5 minutes, or until hot, stirring halfway through.

PREP AND GO: Prep all the veg and place into the glass dish, attach the lid and store in the fridge for up to 24 hours. You can mix the sauce in advance too, and store this separately in the fridge. Once ready to cook, continue from step 2.

MEALS WITH MAX TIPS:
- For more nutrients and variety, add fine green beans or Tenderstem broccoli in with the veg.
- For a lower-carb option, you can replace the potatoes with cauliflower florets and reduce the cooking time slightly.
- If you are cooking for one, halve the ingredients and cook this in the large dish.

One Pot

Calories: 421 **Protein:** 41g **Carbs:** 36g **Fat:** 13g

PREP + GO

Italian Tuna Melt Pasta Bake

If you love a tuna melt, this pasta bake is the ultimate comfort version. Creamy tuna pasta topped with bubbling melted cheese and baked until golden. Thus hearty, satisfying dish is perfect for when you're craving a cosy dinner.

SERVES 2

Cook time: 22 minutes

INGREDIENTS:
- 130g/4½oz dried penne pasta
- 2 x 145g/5oz tins of tuna in spring water, drained
- 300g/10½oz tinned chopped tomatoes
- 2 tbsp tomato purée
- 1 tsp dried oregano
- 1 tsp garlic granules
- 60g/2oz drained tinned sweetcorn
- 40g/1½oz light Cheddar, grated
- 30g/1oz mozzarella
- salt and black pepper
- chopped basil leaves, to garnish

METHOD:
1. Bring a saucepan of salted water to the boil. Add the pasta and cook according to the packet instructions until al dente. Drain well.
2. In a mixing bowl, combine the cooked pasta with the tuna, chopped tomatoes, tomato purée, oregano, garlic granules, sweetcorn and a big pinch of salt and black pepper. Mix until evenly coated.
3. Transfer the mixture to the large glass dish of the portable air fryer, without the tray. Top with the grated Cheddar and tear over the mozzarella.
4. Air fry for 8–10 minutes, or until the cheese is melted, golden and bubbling.
5. Serve in bowls, garnished with fresh basil.

STORE: Cool completely and seal the glass dish with the lid. Store in the fridge for up to 2 days.

REHEAT: Remove the lid and attach the portable air fryer. Use the Recrisp function to heat for 6–7 minutes, or until hot and the cheese is melted.

MEALS WITH MAX TIPS:
- Swap the tuna for shredded cooked chicken for a different flavour.
- For some extra nutrients, add a handful of spinach or chopped peppers to boost your veg.
- If you are cooking for one, halve the ingredients and cook this in the smaller dish.

Calories: 489   **Protein:** 42g   **Carbs:** 62g   **Fat:** 9g

Cajun Cod with Spinach, Roasted Peppers and Turmeric Rice

This dish is all about bold flavours and colour. The Cajun spice gives the cod a lovely kick, while the roasted peppers and golden turmeric rice make it a proper feast for the eyes. It's quick to pull together but tastes like something special.

SERVES 2

Cook time: 20 minutes

INGREDIENTS:
120g/4oz basmati rice
1 tsp ground turmeric
1 tbsp olive oil
1 red pepper, sliced into strips
1 yellow pepper, sliced into strips
2 x 200g/7oz cod fillets
2 tsp Cajun seasoning
handful of baby spinach
salt and black pepper

FOR THE CAJUN YOGURT SAUCE:
4 tbsp Greek yogurt
1 tsp Cajun seasoning
juice of 1 lemon

METHOD:
1. Boil the rice in a saucepan according to the packet instructions, but add a pinch of salt and the turmeric in with the rice before cooking.
2. Add the olive oil and sliced peppers to the large glass dish of the portable air fryer, without the tray. Season with a pinch of salt and cook on the Roast setting for 8 minutes.
3. Stir the peppers, then place the cod fillets in the centre. Sprinkle the fish with Cajun seasoning, salt and black pepper, then roast for a further 8–10 minutes, or until the cod flakes easily.
4. While the fish cooks, mix all the Cajun yogurt sauce ingredients in a small bowl until smooth.
5. Just before serving, stir the spinach through the hot turmeric rice until wilted.
6. Serve the cod over the spinach turmeric rice, with the roasted peppers on the side. Drizzle with the Cajun yogurt sauce, then enjoy. Lovely!

STORE: Best eaten fresh. But if you plan to eat later, cool the cod and peppers completely and seal the glass dish with the lid. Then store in the fridge for up to 1 day. Store the rice separately in the fridge.

REHEAT: Remove the lid and attach the portable air fryer. Use the Recrisp function to heat for 5 minutes, or until hot, stirring halfway through. Reheat the rice in the microwave until piping hot.

MEALS WITH MAX TIPS:
- For a sharper flavour, swap the lemon juice in the sauce for lime juice.
- For extra crunch, you could sprinkle toasted breadcrumbs or toasted pumpkin seeds over the finished dish.
- If you are cooking for one, halve the ingredients and cook this in the large dish.

Calories: 475   **Protein:** 42g   **Carbs:** 53g   **Fat:** 10g

Prawn Tacos with Mango Salsa and Lime Yogurt

Tacos always feel like a treat, and these prawn ones are fresh and fun. The prawns cook quickly in the portable air fryer, while the mango salsa adds sweetness and the lime yogurt keeps it light. A colourful, summery recipe that's perfect for sharing.

SERVES 2

Cook time: 18 minutes

INGREDIENTS:
240g/8½oz raw king prawns, peeled and deveined
1 tbsp olive oil
1 tsp smoked paprika
½ tsp ground cumin
½ tsp garlic powder
4 small soft tortillas
salt and black pepper
coriander leaves, to garnish

FOR THE MANGO SALSA:
1 ripe mango, diced
½ red onion, finely diced
½ red chilli, deseeded and finely diced
juice of 1 lime
handful of fresh coriander, chopped

FOR THE LIME YOGURT:
80g/3oz 0% fat Greek yogurt
grated zest and juice of 1 lime

METHOD:
1. In a bowl, combine the prawns with olive oil, smoked paprika, cumin, garlic powder and a pinch of salt and black pepper. Mix until evenly coated.
2. Arrange the prawns in a single layer on top of the tray in the large glass dish of the portable air fryer. Air fry for 6–8 minutes until pink and slightly charred.
3. Meanwhile, in a separate bowl, mix the mango, red onion, red chilli, lime juice, coriander and a pinch of salt. Set the salsa aside.
4. In another small bowl, stir together the Greek yogurt, lime zest, lime juice and a pinch of salt. Set the lime yogurt aside.
5. Warm the tortillas briefly in the portable air fryer after the prawns are cooked (about 30 seconds). Divide the prawns among the tortillas, top with the mango salsa, drizzle with the lime yogurt and garnish with coriander.

STORE: Best eaten fresh. If eating later, cool the prawns completely and seal the glass dish with the lid. Store in the fridge for up to 24 hours. Store the salsa and yogurt sauce separately in the fridge. Warm the tacos when ready to serve.

REHEAT: Remove the lid and attach the portable air fryer. Use the Recrisp function to heat for 2–3 minutes, or until hot. Then warm your tortilla and build your tacos with the salsa and sauce.

MEALS WITH MAX TIPS:
- Pat the prawns dry with kitchen paper before seasoning. This will help them char and cook better, rather than going soggy.
- If your mango is slightly underripe, mix it with a pinch of sugar to bring out the sweetness.
- If you are cooking for one, halve the ingredients and cook this in the large dish.

One Pot

Calories: 445   **Protein:** 31g   **Carbs:** 54g   **Fat:** 13g

Crispy Salmon Fishcakes with Cucumber Salad and Mint Yogurt

Fishcakes are such a classic, and these salmon ones come out perfectly golden in the portable air fryer. Paired with a refreshing cucumber salad and cooling mint yogurt, they're light, fresh and just as good for lunch as they are for dinner.

SERVES 2

Cook time: 30 minutes

INGREDIENTS:
300g/10½oz Maris piper potatoes, peeled and cut into cubes
300g/10½oz skinless salmon fillet
2 spring onions, finely chopped
2 tbsp chopped parsley
2 tsp grated lemon zest
2 tsp Dijon mustard
2 small eggs, beaten
2 tbsp plain flour
oil spray
salt and black pepper

FOR THE CUCUMBER SALAD:
1 cucumber, thinly sliced
2 tsp white wine vinegar or lemon juice

FOR THE MINT YOGURT SAUCE:
4 tbsp 0% fat Greek yogurt
4 tsp finely chopped mint
4 tsp lemon juice

METHOD:
1. Bring a saucepan of salted water to the boil, add the potato cubes and boil for 12–15 minutes until fork tender. Drain the potatoes, then mash them.
2. While the potato cooks, place the salmon in the large glass dish of the portable air fryer on top of the tray. Air fry for 8–10 minutes, or until cooked through. Remove the salmon and allow to cool slightly, then flake into a large mixing bowl.
3. Add the mashed potatoes, spring onion, parsley, lemon zest, mustard, beaten eggs, salt and black pepper to the bowl with the salmon. Mix well until fully combined.
4. Shape the mixture into four fishcakes, dust lightly with flour, and spray with a little oil.
5. Air fry the fishcakes for 8–10 minutes, flipping halfway through the cooking time, until golden and crispy.
6. Meanwhile, for the cucumber salad, use a potato peeler to thinly slice the cucumber into ribbons. Place into a bowl and mix with vinegar and a big pinch of salt and black pepper.
7. In another small bowl, combine the yogurt, mint, lemon juice and a pinch of salt with 2 tablespoons of water to loosen the sauce.
8. Serve the crispy salmon fishcakes with the cucumber salad on the side and drizzle over the mint yogurt sauce.

STORE: Cool completely and seal the glass dish with the lid. Then store in the fridge for up to 2 days. Store the salad and the sauce separately in the fridge.

REHEAT: Remove the lid and attach the portable air fryer. Use the Recrisp function to heat for 4–5 minutes, or until hot. Serve with the salad and the mint yogurt sauce.

MEALS WITH MAX TIPS:
- Swap the salmon for cod, haddock or tuna for a different twist.
- Add a big pinch of chilli flakes to the fishcake mix for a subtle heat.
- If you are cooking for one, halve the ingredients and cook this in the large dish.

Calories: 428 **Protein:** 46g **Carbs:** 45g **Fat:** 8g

Smoky Paprika Prawn Salad Bowl

PREP + GO

SERVES 2

Cook time: 15 minutes

This is a quick, healthy recipe that is still packed with flavour. The prawns are coated in smoked paprika and cook in minutes, then served over crisp salad with a zesty dressing. It's light but filling, and a great option for a speedy weeknight meal.

INGREDIENTS:
250g/9oz raw king prawns, peeled and deveined
1 tbsp olive oil
2 tsp smoked paprika
1 tsp garlic powder
½ tsp ground cumin
80g/3oz brown rice
100g/3½oz cherry tomatoes, halved
½ cucumber, diced
½ red onion, thinly sliced
2 avocados, sliced
salt and black pepper
chopped parsley, to garnish

FOR THE DRESSING:
6 tbsp 0% fat Greek yogurt
juice of 1 lemon
1 tsp smoked paprika

METHOD:
1. In a bowl, toss the prawns with olive oil, smoked paprika, garlic powder, cumin and a pinch of salt and black pepper until evenly coated.
2. Place the prawns on top of the tray in the large glass dish of the portable air fryer.
3. Air fry for 6–8 minutes until pink and slightly charred.
4. In a small bowl, whisk together the Greek yogurt, lemon juice, smoked paprika and a pinch of salt and black pepper for the dressing. Set aside.
5. Cook the rice according to the packet instructions.
6. Divide the hot rice between two bowls. Arrange the tomatoes, cucumber, red onion and avocado on top. Add the cooked prawns, drizzle with the dressing and sprinkle with chopped parsley to garnish.

STORE: Best eaten fresh. If eating later, cool the prawns completely, and seal the glass dish with the lid. Store in the fridge for up to 24 hours. Store the salad and dressing separately. Cook the rice when ready to serve.

REHEAT: Remove the lid and attach the portable air fryer. Use the Recrisp function to heat for 2–3 minutes, or until hot. While it reheats, microwave the rice.

PREP AND GO: Prep to the end of step 2, then attach the lid and store in the fridge for up to 24 hours. If you like, you can prep the dressing in advance and store this separately in the fridge. Once ready to cook, attach to the portable air fryer and continue from step 3.

MEALS WITH MAX TIPS:
- If you've got time, let the prawns sit in the spices for 10 minutes before cooking so the flavour soaks in.
- Pat the prawns dry with kitchen paper before seasoning. This will help them char and cook better, rather than going soggy.
- If you are cooking for one, halve the ingredients and cook this in the smaller dish.
- You can use microwave rice to save time, if you want.

Calories: 478   **Protein:** 31g   **Carbs:** 45g   **Fat:** 21g

Chilli Lemon Salmon with Corn Salsa and Zesty Rice

This is one of my fiancé's favourite salmon recipes. The chilli and lemon make the fish zingy and bright, while the corn salsa adds crunch and sweetness. Served with fluffy zesty rice, it's a balanced meal that's bursting with flavour.

SERVES 2

Cook time: 15 minutes

INGREDIENTS:
2 x 150g/5¼oz skinless salmon fillets
1 tsp olive oil
1 tsp chilli flakes
1 tsp smoked paprika
1 tsp garlic granules
grated zest of 1 lemon
salt and black pepper

FOR THE CORN SALSA:
200g/7oz drained tinned sweetcorn
8 cherry tomatoes, diced
½ red onion, finely diced
2 tbsp chopped coriander
juice of 1 lime

FOR THE ZESTY RICE:
80g/3oz basmati rice
grated zest of 1 lime
2 tbsp chopped coriander

METHOD:
1. Rub the salmon fillets with the olive oil, chilli flakes, smoked paprika, garlic granules, lemon zest, salt and black pepper.
2. Place the salmon into the large glass dish of the portable air fryer, on top of the tray.
3. Air fry for 8–10 minutes, or until cooked to your liking.
4. Meanwhile, make the corn salsa. In a small bowl, mix the sweetcorn, cherry tomatoes, red onion, coriander, lime juice and some salt and black pepper. Set aside.
5. Cook the rice according to the packet instructions, then stir in the lime zest and coriander.
6. Serve the salmon with the zesty rice and the corn salsa, then enjoy. Lovely!

STORE: Best eaten fresh. But if you plan to eat later, cool completely and seal the glass dish with the lid. Store the salmon, salsa and zesty rice separately in the fridge for up to 48 hours.

REHEAT: Remove the lid and attach the portable air fryer. Use the Recrisp function to heat for 3–4 minutes, or until hot. Prep the rice as per the instructions above and serve with your salsa.

PREP AND GO: Prep up to the end of step 2, attach the lid and then store in the fridge for up to 24 hours. Once ready to cook, attach to the portable air fryer and continue from step 3. You can also prep the salsa in advance and store this separately, or you can prep it fresh while the salmon cooks as per the recipe.

MEALS WITH MAX TIPS:
- Swap the salmon for prawns and reduce the cooking time to 5–6 minutes.
- Add diced avocado to the salsa for a creamy twist and to boost the healthy fats. However, do consider that the avocado will increase the calories.
- If you are cooking for one, halve the ingredients and cook this in the large dish.
- You can use microwave rice to save time, if you want.

Calories: 485 **Protein:** 37g **Carbs:** 57g **Fat:** 14g

Vegetarian dishes shine in the air fryer. The high heat brings out incredible flavour and crispness in vegetables, all while keeping prep minimal. These recipes are packed with colour, crunch and comfort and whether you're cooking for yourself or sharing, they'll leave you full and happy without feeling heavy. My favourite recipe from this section is the Crispy Cheesy Veggie Quesadilla (page 100) – melty, golden and proof that simple ingredients can taste amazing when cooked just right.

Falafel Wrap with Pickled Red Onion and Garlic Yogurt	98
Crispy Cheesy Veggie Quesadilla	100
Ratatouille Traybake with Halloumi and Balsamic Glaze	102
Indian Paneer and Pepper Bake with Coriander Chutney	104
Baked Ricotta and Spinach Pasta with a Crispy Cheesy Crust	106
Crispy Gnocchi with Tomatoes and Pesto	108
Cherry Tomato, Feta and Basil Pasta Bake	110

Vegetarian

06

Falafel Wrap with Pickled Red Onion and Garlic Yogurt

I love this recipe because it's fresh, punchy and full of texture. The falafel is crisp on the outside and fluffy inside, the pickled onion adds sharpness, and the garlic yogurt ties everything together. Wrapped up in a tortilla, it's a satisfying lunch or dinner that's just as good on the go.

SERVES 2

Cook time: 20 minutes

INGREDIENTS:
- 300g/10½oz drained tinned chickpeas, rinsed
- 2 small garlic cloves
- 4 tbsp parsley leaves
- 2 tbsp plain flour
- 2 tsp ground cumin
- 2 tsp ground coriander
- oil spray
- 2 tortilla wraps
- handful of mixed salad leaves
- 1 tomato, sliced
- ½ cucumber, thinly sliced
- salt and black pepper

FOR THE PICKLED RED ONION:
- ½ small red onion, thinly sliced
- 2 tbsp white wine vinegar

FOR THE GARLIC YOGURT SAUCE:
- 100g/3½oz 0% fat Greek yogurt
- 1 small garlic clove, grated

METHOD:
1. Start by making the pickled red onion. In a small bowl, combine the red onion, vinegar and a big pinch of salt. Set aside for at least 15 minutes.
2. For the garlic yogurt sauce, mix the yogurt, garlic and big pinch of salt in another small bowl. Keep cool in the fridge.
3. In a food processor or blender, pulse the chickpeas, garlic, parsley, flour, cumin, coriander, salt and black pepper until you have a slightly chunky paste. Take care not to overblend.
4. Form the mixture into eight small balls and flatten slightly.
5. Place the falafel into the large glass dish of the portable air fryer, on top of the tray.
6. Spray them lightly with oil and cook on the Roast setting for 10–12 minutes, flipping halfway through the cooking time, until golden and crispy.
7. Warm the wraps in the air fryer for the final 1 minute of cooking.
8. Spread the garlic yogurt over the wraps, top with salad leaves, tomato, cucumber, falafels and drained pickled onion. Roll up tightly and serve.

STORE: Cool the falafel completely and seal the glass dish with the lid. Then store in the fridge for up to 3 days. For best results, do not wrap it up before storing. Store the falafel in the glass dish, then store the pickled onion, sauce and salad separately.

REHEAT: Remove the lid and attach the portable air fryer. Use the Recrisp function to heat for 4–5 minutes, or until hot. Then wrap the falafel up with the salad, sauce and pickled onion.

PREP AND GO: To prep this ahead of time, prep up to step 5 and attach the lid to the portable air fryer dish. Store in the fridge for up to 24 hours. Store the garlic sauce and pickled onion separately in the fridge. Continue from step 6 when you're ready to eat.

MEALS WITH MAX TIPS:
- For extra crunch, toss the falafel in 2 teaspoons of sesame seeds before air frying.
- For a slightly different flavour, try swapping the parsley for coriander.
- If you are cooking for one, halve the ingredients and cook this in the smaller dish.

One Pot

Calories: 476 **Protein:** 23g **Carbs:** 78g **Fat:** 8g

Crispy Cheesy Veggie Quesadilla

This is one of those recipes that proves simple is often best. Gooey melted cheese, crisp golden tortillas and plenty of colourful veg make it a total winner. It's quick to throw together and always feels fun to eat – especially with salsa or guacamole on the side.

SERVES 1

Cook time: 15 minutes

INGREDIENTS:
1 tbsp pesto
1 tortilla wrap
½ red pepper, finely diced
½ onion, finely diced
25g/1oz mozzarella
handful of baby spinach
2 tbsp ricotta
oil spray
salt and black pepper

METHOD:
1. Spread the pesto on one half of the wrap. Top with the diced veg, mozzarella, spinach and ricotta.
2. Season with salt and black pepper, then fold the wrap in half. If your wraps are too big to fit in the air fryer, cut it in half to create two quarters.
3. Place into the glass dish of the portable air fryer, on top of the tray. Spray with a little oil. Cook for 8 minutes until the mozzarella has melted and the wrap is crispy.
4. Serve hot and enjoy. Lovely!

STORE: Cool completely and seal the glass dish with the lid. Then store in the fridge for up to 3 days.

REHEAT: Remove the lid and attach the portable air fryer. Use the Recrisp function to heat for 5–6 minutes, or until hot.

MEALS WITH MAX TIPS:
- Add a pinch of chilli flakes for some heat.
- Feel free to mix up the cheese! Cream cheese or mascarpone work great as an alternative to the ricotta.
- If you are cooking for more than one, it is best to cook the quesadillas in batches to avoid overcrowding the air fryer.

One Pot

Calories: 400   **Protein:** 18g   **Carbs:** 40g   **Fat:** 15g

PREP + GO

Ratatouille Traybake with Halloumi and Balsamic Glaze

This dish is all about big Mediterranean flavours. The roasted vegetables get soft and caramelised, the halloumi adds salty richness and a drizzle of balsamic glaze makes it sing. It's hearty enough to serve as a main, but works just as well as a vibrant side for sharing.

SERVES 2

Cook time: 25 minutes

INGREDIENTS:
1 tbsp olive oil
1 small red onion, cut into wedges
1 courgette, sliced into 1cm/½in rounds
1 small aubergine, cut into 2cm/¾in cubes
1 red pepper, cut into 2cm/¾in chunks
2 small tomatoes, cut into wedges
2 garlic cloves, grated
1 tsp dried oregano
200g/7oz halloumi, sliced into 1cm/½in pieces
2 tbsp balsamic glaze
salt and black pepper
basil leaves, to garnish

METHOD:
1. Add the olive oil, red onion, courgette, aubergine, red pepper, tomatoes, garlic, oregano and a pig pinch of salt and black pepper to the large glass dish of the portable air fryer, without the tray. Mix well until the veg is fully coated.
2. Cook on the Roast setting for 15 minutes, stirring halfway through the cooking time.
3. Add the halloumi slices on top of the vegetables and roast for a further 6-7 minutes until the cheese is golden and the vegetables are tender.
4. Divide the veg between two plates, layer on the halloumi and then drizzle the balsamic glaze over the top. Garnish with some fresh basil leaves and enjoy!

STORE: Cool completely and seal the glass dish with the lid. Then store in the fridge for up to 2 days.

REHEAT: Remove the lid and attach the portable air fryer. Use the Recrisp function to heat for 4–5 minutes, or until hot.

PREP AND GO: Prep step 1, but don't add the oil. Attach the lid and store in the fridge for up to 24 hours. When you're ready to eat, add the oil and mix well, then continue with the remaining steps.

MEALS WITH MAX TIPS:
- Add 1 teaspoon of smoked paprika with the oregano for extra depth.
- Try swapping the halloumi for feta: just crumble it over the veg after cooking and then drizzle with the balsamic glaze.
- If you are cooking for one, halve the ingredients and cook this in the large dish.

One Pot

Calories: 449   **Protein:** 24g   **Carbs:** 19g   **Fat:** 31g

Indian Paneer and Pepper Bake with Coriander Chutney

Paneer is such a versatile cheese, and here it soaks up all the Indian-inspired spices beautifully. Roasted with peppers until golden, it's served with a fresh, zesty coriander chutney that really lifts the dish. It's warming, colourful and one of my favourite meat-free meals.

SERVES 2

Cook time: 25 minutes

INGREDIENTS:
1 tbsp olive oil
1 small red onion, cut into thin wedges
1 red pepper, sliced into strips
1 yellow pepper, sliced into strips
200g/7oz paneer, cut into 2cm/¾in cubes

FOR THE CURRY SAUCE:
150g/5¼oz passata
2 tbsp Greek yogurt
1 tsp garam masala
1 tsp ground cumin
½ tsp ground turmeric
salt and black pepper

FOR THE CORIANDER CHUTNEY:
handful of coriander leaves
1 green chilli
2 tbsp Greek yogurt
juice of 1 lime

METHOD:
1. In a small bowl, whisk all the sauce ingredients together until smooth and fully combined. Set aside.
2. Add the olive oil, onion, peppers and paneer to the large glass dish of the portable air fryer, without the tray. Pour over the sauce and mix well to coat everything evenly.
3. Cook on the Roast setting for 16–18 minutes, stirring halfway through the cooking time, until the vegetables are tender and the paneer is golden with a lightly caramelised sauce coating.
4. While the bake cooks, make the chutney. In a small blender, blitz the coriander, green chilli, yogurt, lime juice and a big pinch of salt until smooth.
5. Serve the paneer and pepper bake hot, with the coriander chutney drizzled over the top. Garnish with a few coriander leaves and enjoy!

STORE: Cool completely and seal the glass dish with the lid. Then store in the fridge for up to 2 days. Store the chutney separately in the fridge.

REHEAT: Remove the lid and attach the portable air fryer. Use the Recrisp function to heat for 5–6 minutes, or until hot.

PREP AND GO: Prep up to the end of step 2, attach the lid and store in the fridge for up to 24 hours. Once ready to cook, attach to the portable air fryer and continue from step 3.

MEALS WITH MAX TIPS:
- If you like it extra saucy, double the sauce quantities.
- For a more filling meal, serve over rice for a quick paneer curry or serve with a naan on the side.
- If you are cooking for one, halve the ingredients and cook this in the large dish.

One Pot

Calories: 471   **Protein:** 25g   **Carbs:** 14g   **Fat:** 31g

Baked Ricotta and Spinach Pasta with a Crispy Cheesy Crust

This pasta bake feels like pure comfort food, but with a lighter twist. The ricotta and spinach make the filling creamy and nourishing, while the golden cheesy crust on top is impossible to resist. It's the kind of dish you'll want to serve bubbling straight from the oven.

SERVES 2

Cook time: 20 minutes

INGREDIENTS:
120g/4oz dried penne pasta
150g/5¼oz ricotta
100g/3½oz baby spinach
2 small garlic cloves, grated
40g/1½oz grated Parmesan or vegetarian hard cheese
40g/1½oz grated mozzarella cheese, for topping
salt and black pepper
green salad, to serve

METHOD:
1. Bring a saucepan of salted water to the boil and cook the pasta until just al dente (about 10 minutes). Drain well, but save a few tablespoons of pasta water.
2. In a mixing bowl, combine the cooked pasta, reserved pasta water, ricotta, spinach, garlic, half the Parmesan and a big pinch of salt and black pepper. Stir until evenly mixed.
3. Transfer the mixture to the glass dish of the portable air fryer, without the tray.
4. Sprinkle the mozzarella and remaining Parmesan evenly over the top to form a crust.
5. Cook on the Roast setting for 8–10 minutes until the top is golden and crisp.
6. Serve hot with a green side salad, if liked.

STORE: Cool completely and seal the glass dish with the lid. Then store in the fridge for up to 2 days.

REHEAT: Remove the lid and attach the portable air fryer. Use the Recrisp function to heat for 5 minutes, or until hot.

MEALS WITH MAX TIPS:
- Mix 2 teaspoons of chopped basil or parsley into the ricotta for a herby flavour.
- Sprinkle 2 tablespoons of breadcrumbs over the cheese topping before baking for an extra crispy crust.
- If you are cooking for one, halve the ingredients and cook this in the smaller dish.

One Pot

Calories: 420   **Protein:** 27g   **Carbs:** 42g   **Fat:** 17g

Crispy Gnocchi with Tomatoes and Pesto

If you've never had gnocchi in the air fryer, this recipe will be a game changer. The gnocchi go golden and crisp on the outside while staying soft inside, and tossing them with roasted tomatoes and pesto makes it incredibly moreish. It's fast, comforting and full of flavour.

SERVES 2

Cook time: 25 minutes

INGREDIENTS:
250g/9oz fresh gnocchi
1 tbsp olive oil
200g/7oz cherry tomatoes, halved
2 tbsp green pesto
20g/¾oz Parmesan or vegetarian hard cheese, finely grated
salt and black pepper
basil leaves, to garnish

METHOD:
1. Add the gnocchi, olive oil, cherry tomatoes and a big pinch of salt and black pepper to the large glass dish of the portable air fryer, without the tray. Mix well to coat.
2. Air fry for 12–14 minutes, stirring halfway through the cooking time, until the gnocchi are golden and crisp on the outside and the tomatoes are softened and juicy.
3. Add the pesto to the dish and then mix well until the tomatoes and gnocchi are evenly coated.
4. Divide between two plates, sprinkle with the grated Parmesan and garnish with fresh basil leaves. Lovely!

STORE: Cool the gnocchi completely and seal the glass dish with the lid. Then store in the fridge for up to 2 days. If cooking to eat later, it would be best to add the pesto just before serving.

REHEAT: Remove the lid and attach the portable air fryer. Use the Recrisp function to heat for 5 minutes, or until hot. Stir in the pesto, then serve.

MEALS WITH MAX TIPS:
- For a little extra protein, you could add some mozzarella pearls before serving.
- Swap pesto for a sun-dried tomato paste for a richer, sweeter flavour.
- If you are cooking for one, halve the ingredients and cook this in the large dish.

One Pot

Calories: 471   **Protein:** 25g   **Carbs:** 14g   **Fat:** 31g

Cherry Tomato, Feta and Basil Pasta Bake

This one is summer in a pasta bake: sweet roasted cherry tomatoes, tangy feta and fresh basil. It's simple, colourful and has all the flavours of a Caprese salad, but in a hearty, traybake form. Perfect for when you want something easy but packed with flavour.

SERVES 2

Cook time: 22 minutes

INGREDIENTS:
120g/4oz dried fusilli pasta
1 tbsp olive oil
200g/7oz cherry tomatoes, halved
2 garlic cloves, grated
70g/2½oz feta, crumbled
2 tbsp Greek yogurt
6 tbsp passata
handful of basil leaves, torn, plus extra leaves to garnish
30g/1oz Parmesan or vegetarian hard cheese, grated, plus extra to serve
salt and black pepper

METHOD:
1. Bring a saucepan of salted water to the boil and cook the pasta until just al dente (about 10 minutes). Drain well but save a few tablespoons of pasta water.
2. In a mixing bowl, combine the cooked pasta, reserved pasta water, olive oil, cherry tomatoes, garlic, feta, Greek yogurt, passata, torn basil and a big pinch of salt and pepper. Stir until fully combined.
3. Transfer the mixture to the large glass dish of the portable air fryer, without the tray. Cook on the Roast setting for 6 minutes.
4. Stir the pasta well, then sprinkle over the Parmesan. Cook for a further 6–7 minutes until the cheese is golden and the tomatoes are soft and saucy.
5. Serve garnished with extra basil and more grated Parmesan, if liked.

STORE: Cool completely and seal the glass dish with the lid. Then store in the fridge for up to 2 days.

REHEAT: Remove the lid and attach the portable air fryer. Use the Recrisp function to heat for 4–5 minutes, or until hot. You can mix in a small splash of water before reheating to help loosen it a little.

MEALS WITH MAX TIPS:
- To boost the protein a little, stir in 100g/3½oz of cooked cannellini beans before baking.
- Add 1 teaspoon of lemon zest just before serving to brighten the flavour
- If you are cooking for one, halve the ingredients and cook this in the smaller dish.

Calories: 438 **Protein:** 16g **Carbs:** 41g **Fat:** 21g

These vegan recipes are all about big flavour and satisfying texture – proof that plant-based cooking can be anything but bland. The air fryer turns veg and tofu crisp and caramelised with no fuss. Mix and match ingredients, play with seasonings and don't be afraid to experiment – these dishes are designed to be as flexible as they are delicious. If you are in the mood for something sweet, smoky and packed with warm, vibrant flavours turn to the Moroccan-spiced Veg Tray with Chickpeas and Apricots (page 126).

BBQ Jackfruit Wrap with Slaw and Pickles	114
Crispy Chickpea and Sweet Potato Salad	116
Lemon Roasted Cauliflower Salad with Tahini Dressing	118
Spicy Black Bean Quesadillas with Guacamole and Salsa	120
Teriyaki Tofu Bowl with Edamame and Rice	122
Tofu, Sweet Potato and Spinach Curry Bake	124
Moroccan-spiced Veg Tray with Chickpeas and Apricots	126

Vegan

07

BBQ Jackfruit Wrap with Slaw and Pickles

Jackfruit is a brilliant plant-based swap for pulled pork, and in this recipe, it soaks up all the sweet, smoky BBQ flavour. Wrapped up with crunchy slaw and sharp pickles, it's messy, delicious and one of those vegan recipes everyone ends up loving.

SERVES 2

Cook time: 20 minutes

INGREDIENTS:
- 250g/9oz tin of young green jackfruit, shredded
- 2 tsp olive oil
- 1 tsp smoked paprika
- 1 tsp garlic powder
- 1 tsp onion granules
- 4 tbsp BBQ sauce, plus extra for brushing
- 2 tortilla wraps
- salt and black pepper
- pickled gherkins, to serve

FOR THE SLAW:
- 160g/5½oz red cabbage, thinly sliced
- ½ carrot, grated
- 2 tbsp light mayo
- 2 tsp apple cider vinegar

METHOD:
1. Mix the shredded jackfruit with the oil, paprika, garlic powder, onion granules, salt and black pepper.
2. Then place directly into the bottom of the large glass dish of the portable air fryer, without the tray.
3. Cook on the Roast setting for 12 minutes, stirring halfway through the cooking time.
4. Meanwhile, mix all the slaw ingredients together in a bowl and season with salt and pepper. Stir the BBQ sauce into the jackfruit, then roast for a further 3–4 minutes until edges caramelise.
5. Warm the tortillas in your microwave or air fryer for 30 seconds. Now it's time to build your wrap! Add the BBQ jackfruit, slaw and pickles. Wrap tightly, slice in half and enjoy. Lovely!

STORE: Cool the BBQ jackfruit completely and seal the glass dish with the lid. Then store in the fridge for up to 3 days. Store the coleslaw in a separate airtight container. Heat the wraps when serving.

REHEAT: Remove the lid and attach the portable air fryer. Use the Recrisp function to heat for 5–6 minutes, or until hot. Then wrap it up with your coleslaw and pickles!

PREP AND GO: To prep this ahead of time, follow the above instructions to the end of step 2 and then attach the storage lid. Store in the fridge for up to 3 days. Once ready to cook, attach to the portable air fryer and continue from step 3. You can prep the coleslaw in advance and store separately, but for best results, make this fresh while the jackfruit cooks.

MEALS WITH MAX TIPS:
- After draining the jackfruit, gently press between kitchen paper to remove excess moisture.
- If you prefer a crispy wrap, place it into the air fryer for a few minutes after wrapping it up.
- If you are cooking for one, halve the ingredients and cook this in the smaller dish.

One Pot

Calories: 351 **Protein:** 8g **Carbs:** 70g **Fat:** 4g

Crispy Chickpea and Sweet Potato Salad

This salad is anything but boring. The chickpeas go wonderfully crisp in the portable air fryer, the roasted sweet potato adds natural sweetness and everything is finished with a zingy dressing. It's hearty enough to be a main but still feels light and fresh.

SERVES 2
Cook time: 25 minutes

INGREDIENTS:
300g/10½oz drained tinned chickpeas, rinsed
400g/14oz sweet potato, peeled and cut into small cubes
1 tbsp olive oil
2 tsp smoked paprika
1 tsp garlic granules
1 tsp ground cumin
½ cucumber, diced
1 red onion, thinly sliced
12 cherry tomatoes, halved
handful of mixed salad leaves
salt and black pepper

FOR THE DRESSING:
2 tbsp 0% vegan Greek-style yogurt
2 tsp lemon juice
2 tsp agave nectar

METHOD:
1. Pat the chickpeas dry with kitchen paper and then place them into a bowl with the sweet potato cubes. Add the oil, smoked paprika, garlic granules, ground cumin and a pinch of salt and pepper.
2. Mix until the sweet potato and chickpeas are fully coated and then place them into the large glass dish of the portable air fryer, on top of the tray.
3. Air fry for 18-20 minutes, stirring halfway through the cooking time.
4. Meanwhile, combine the cucumber, red onion and tomatoes in a bowl and then mix them in with the salad leaves.
5. Whisk together all the dressing ingredients in a small bowl until smooth. Season with salt and pepper.
6. Once the sweet potato and chickpeas are golden and crispy, scatter them on top of the salad. Drizzle over the dressing and then enjoy. Lovely!

STORE: Cool the sweet potato and chickpeas completely and seal the glass dish with the lid. Then store in the fridge for up to 3 days. Build the salad when you're ready to eat.

REHEAT: Remove the lid and attach the portable air fryer. Use the Recrisp function to heat for 5 minutes, or until hot and crispy. Then build your salad.

PREP AND GO: To prep this ahead of time, follow the above instructions to the end of step 2 and then attach the storage lid. Store in the fridge for up to 2 days. Once ready to cook, attach to the portable air fryer and continue from step 3.

MEALS WITH MAX TIPS:
- Swap the vegan Greek-style yogurt for tahini in the dressing for a creamier, richer option.
- Add crumbled vegan feta cheese for more protein and a salty kick.
- If you are cooking for one, halve the ingredients and cook this in the large dish.

One Pot

Calories: 495   **Protein:** 17g   **Carbs:** 84g   **Fat:** 11g

Lemon Roasted Cauliflower Salad with Tahini Dressing

I love the balance of flavours in this dish – the roasted cauliflower has a zesty lemon kick, the pomegranate brings bursts of sweetness and the creamy tahini dressing ties it all together. It's vibrant, colourful and perfect for when you want something a bit different.

SERVES 2

Cook time: 25 minutes

INGREDIENTS:
- 500g/1lb 2oz cauliflower florets
- 2 tsp olive oil
- grated zest of 1 lemon
- 2 garlic cloves, grated
- 1 tsp ground cumin
- 1 tsp smoked paprika
- handful of parsley and mint, chopped
- 40g/1½oz toasted almonds, roughly chopped
- handful of mixed salad leaves
- ½ cucumber, diced
- 100g/3½oz pomegranate seeds
- salt and black pepper

FOR THE DRESSING:
- 2 tbsp tahini
- 2 tbsp 0% vegan Greek yogurt
- 2 tbsp lemon juice
- 2 tsp maple syrup

METHOD:
1. Add the cauliflower florets to a mixing bowl. Drizzle with the olive oil, then sprinkle over the lemon zest, garlic, cumin, smoked paprika and a big pinch of salt and pepper. Mix until the cauliflower is fully coated.
2. Place the cauliflower into the large glass dish of the portable air fryer, with the tray, arranging them in a single layer on top of the tray.
3. Cook on the Roast setting for 18–20 minutes, stirring halfway through the cooking time, until golden, crispy and slightly charred at the edges.
4. In a small bowl, whisk together the tahini, Greek yogurt, lemon juice and maple syrup with a pinch of salt. Gradually whisk in 4 tablespoons of cold water until it's smooth and pourable.
5. Once the cauliflower is cooked, toss it with the fresh herbs and half the toasted almonds.
6. To serve, divide the salad leaves and cucumber between two bowls, top with the lemon roasted cauliflower, scatter over the remaining almonds and the pomegranate seeds, and drizzle with the creamy tahini dressing. Lovely!

STORE: Cool the cauliflower completely and seal the glass dish with the lid. Then store in the fridge for up to 3 days. Store the dressing separately. Build the salad when you're ready to eat.

REHEAT: Remove the lid and attach the portable air fryer. Use the Recrisp function to heat for 3 minutes, or until hot. Then assemble the salad and add the dressing.

PREP AND GO: To prep this ahead of time, prep up to step 2 and then add the lid. Store it in the fridge for up to 48 hours. You can also mix the dressing ingredients in advance and store this separately in the fridge. Once ready to cook, attach to the portable air fryer and continue from step 3.

MEALS WITH MAX TIPS:
- Swap the almonds for pistachios for extra colour and flavour.
- Add some sliced red chilli or chilli flakes for some heat.
- If you are cooking for one, halve the ingredients and cook this in the large dish.

One Pot

Calories: 439 **Protein:** 11g **Carbs:** 31g **Fat:** 30g

Spicy Black Bean Quesadillas with Guacamole and Salsa

These quesadillas are simple, spicy and so satisfying. The black beans are seasoned with warming spices, then wrapped in tortillas with cheese and cooked until crisp. Served with guacamole and salsa, this is the kind of recipe you'll come back to again and again.

SERVES 1

Cook time: 22 minutes

INGREDIENTS:
- ½ red onion, finely diced
- 1 small red chilli, deseeded and finely chopped
- 1 garlic clove, grated
- oil spray
- 90g/3oz drained tinned black beans, rinsed
- ½ tsp ground cumin
- ½ tsp smoked paprika
- 2 tsp tomato purée
- 2 small soft flour tortillas
- 25g/1oz vegan cheese, grated
- salt and black pepper

FOR THE GUACAMOLE:
- 1/3 ripe avocado
- 1 tsp lime juice

FOR THE SALSA:
- 4 cherry tomatoes, finely diced
- ¼ red onion, finely diced
- 1 tsp lime juice
- 1 tbsp chopped coriander

METHOD:
1. Place the onion, chilli and garlic into the large glass dish of the portable air fryer, without the tray, with a light spray of oil. Air fry for 3–4 minutes until softened.
2. Add the black beans, cumin, smoked paprika, tomato purée, a pinch of salt and pepper and 1 tablespoon of water directly to the dish. Stir and lightly mash the beans with a fork until partly crushed.
3. Air fry for a further 4 minutes to heat through, then remove the mixture and set aside.
4. Lay one tortilla on a chopping board, spread over the bean mixture, sprinkle with vegan cheese and top with the second tortilla. Press down gently.
5. Lightly spray both sides of the quesadilla with oil and place back into the portable air fryer, on top of the tray.
6. Air fry for 6 minutes, flipping halfway through the cooking time, until golden and crisp.
7. Meanwhile, using a fork, mash the avocado with the lime juice and a pinch of salt to make the guacamole. Combine the tomatoes, red onion, lime juice, coriander and a pinch of salt for the salsa.
8. Once golden and crispy, slice the quesadilla into wedges and serve hot with the guacamole and salsa. Then enjoy!

STORE: Cool the quesadilla completely and seal the glass dish with the lid. Then store in the fridge for up to 2 days. Store the salsa and guacamole separately.

REHEAT: Remove the lid and attach the portable air fryer. Use the Recrisp function to heat for 4 minutes, or until hot and crispy. Serve with the guacamole and salsa.

MEALS WITH MAX TIPS:
- Add sweetcorn or diced peppers to the bean filling before cooking for extra flavour and colour.
- For an extra kick, drizzle hot sauce over the filling before sealing the quesadilla. If you are cooking for more than one, it is best to cook the quesadilla in batches to avoid overcrowding the air fryer.

One Pot

Calories: 483 **Protein:** 14g **Carbs:** 68g **Fat:** 18g

Teriyaki Tofu Bowl with Edamame and Rice

SERVES 2

Cook time: 20 minutes

This is one of my favourite high-protein vegan meals. The tofu turns golden and crisp, then gets coated in a sticky homemade teriyaki sauce. Paired with rice, edamame and spring onions, it's fresh, filling and perfect for meal prep.

INGREDIENTS:
300g/10½oz extra-firm tofu, drained and patted dry
2 tsp cornflour
oil spray
130g/4½oz frozen edamame beans
80g/3oz rice
4 spring onions, sliced
2 tsp sesame seeds
salt and black pepper

FOR THE TERIYAKI SAUCE:
4 tbsp reduced-salt soy sauce
4 tsp maple syrup
2 tbsp rice vinegar
1 tsp sesame oil
1 tsp grated fresh ginger
2 small garlic cloves, grated
1 tsp cornflour

METHOD:
1. Cut the tofu into bite-sized cubes. Add to a mixing bowl with the cornflour and a big pinch of salt and black pepper, and mix until it is coated evenly.
2. Place the tray into the large glass dish of the portable air fryer with the tray, and arrange the tofu in a single layer on top of the tray.
3. Air fry for 10–12 minutes, flipping halfway through the cooking time, until golden and crisp.
4. While the tofu cooks, place the frozen edamame in a heatproof bowl, cover with boiling water, and leave for 4 minutes. Drain in a colander and set aside.
5. In a small microwave-safe bowl, whisk together the teriyaki sauce ingredients with 4 tablespoons of water. Microwave for 20–30 seconds until hot, then stir it well. It should start to thicken slightly as it cools down.
6. Cook the rice according to the packet instructions.
7. When the tofu is done, remove the tray and put the tofu directly into the bottom of the glass dish of the portable air fryer. Pour over the teriyaki sauce and toss to coat evenly. Then air fry for a further 1 minute.
8. To serve, divide the rice between two bowls, top with teriyaki tofu, edamame and sliced spring onions, then sprinkle with sesame seeds and enjoy.

STORE: Cool the tofu completely and seal the glass dish with the lid. Then store in the fridge for up to 3 days. It's best to prepare the edamame, rice and spring onions when serving.

REHEAT: Remove the lid and attach the portable air fryer. Use the Recrisp function to heat for 4 minutes, or until hot. While it reheats, cook the rice, prep the edamame and slice the spring onions.

PREP AND GO: To make this ahead of time, prep up to step 2 and then add the lid. Store it in the fridge for up to 24 hours. You can also mix the teriyaki ingredients in advance and store this separately in the fridge. Once ready to cook, attach to the portable air fryer and continue from step 3.

MEALS WITH MAX TIPS:
- Add steamed broccoli or stir-fried peppers for extra colour and nutrition.
- Feel free to swap edamame for sugar snap peas or green beans if you prefer.
- If you are cooking for one, halve the ingredients and cook this in the large dish.
- You can use microwave rice to save time, if you want.

Calories: 497 **Protein:** 28g **Carbs:** 57g **Fat:** 17g

Tofu, Sweet Potato and Spinach Curry Bake

This curry bake is all about cosy, comforting flavours. The tofu and sweet potato soak up the spiced sauce, while the spinach keeps it fresh and vibrant. Everything bakes together so the flavours really develop, making it a great dish for colder evenings.

SERVES 2

Cook time: 30 minutes

INGREDIENTS:
1 tbsp coconut oil
1 onion, finely diced
2 garlic cloves, grated
1 tbsp mild curry powder
1 tsp ground cumin
½ tsp ground turmeric
360g/12½oz sweet potato, peeled and cut into 2cm/¾in cubes
360g/12½oz extra-firm tofu, pressed and diced into 2cm/¾in cubes
200ml/7fl oz light coconut milk
150g/5¼oz baby spinach
150g/5¼oz cherry tomatoes, halved
salt and black pepper
chopped coriander, to garnish

METHOD:
1. Add the coconut oil to the large glass dish of the portable air fryer, without the tray, and cook for 2 minutes on the Roast setting to allow it to heat up.
2. Stir in the onion and garlic, then cook on the Roast setting for 2 minutes until softened.
3. Add the curry powder, cumin and turmeric, mix well and then cook for a further 1 minute.
4. Stir in the sweet potato and tofu cubes, coating well in the spices.
5. Pour in the coconut milk, season with salt and black pepper, and stir to combine.
6. Cook on the Roast setting for 20 minutes, stirring halfway through the cooking time to ensure even cooking.
7. Add the spinach and cherry tomatoes, stir and then roast for a further 5 minutes until the sweet potatoes are tender and the spinach has wilted.
8. Serve garnished with fresh coriander and then enjoy. Lovely!

STORE: Cool completely and seal the glass dish with the lid. Then store in the fridge for up to 3 days.

REHEAT: Remove the lid and attach the portable air fryer. Use the Recrisp function to heat for 6 minutes, or until hot, stirring halfway through.

MEALS WITH MAX TIPS:
- You could swap spinach for kale, but be sure to add it earlier, so it softens fully.
- As an alternative protein source, you can replace the tofu with chickpeas, tempeh or seitan.
- If you are cooking for one, halve the ingredients and cook this in the large dish.

One Pot

Calories: 487 **Protein:** 25g **Carbs:** 41g **Fat:** 25g

Moroccan-spiced Veg Tray with Chickpeas and Apricots

This traybake is packed with warm Moroccan spices, colourful veg and sweet pops of apricot. The chickpeas add protein and crunch, making it a complete meal in one dish. It's fragrant, hearty and tastes just as good the next day.

SERVES 2

Cook time: 30 minutes

INGREDIENTS:
- 1 tbsp olive oil
- 1 small red onion, cut into wedges
- 1 small courgette, cut into 2cm/¾in chunks
- 1 red pepper, cut into 2cm/¾in pieces
- 300g/10½oz sweet potatoes, peeled and cut into 2cm/¾in cubes
- 1 carrot, sliced into 1cm/½in rounds
- 1 tsp ground cumin
- 1 tsp ground coriander
- 1 tsp smoked paprika
- ½ tsp ground cinnamon
- 150g/5¼oz tinned tomatoes
- 125g/4oz drained tinned chickpeas, rinsed
- 2 dried apricots, chopped
- salt and black pepper
- finely chopped parsley, to garnish
- lemon wedges, to serve

METHOD:
1. Add the olive oil, onion, courgette, red pepper, sweet potato and carrot to the large glass dish of the portable air fryer, without the tray.
2. Sprinkle over the cumin, coriander, smoked paprika and cinnamon. Season with salt and black pepper, then mix well until the veg is evenly coated.
3. Cook on the Roast setting for 15 minutes, stirring halfway through the cooking time.
4. Add the tinned tomatoes, chickpeas and chopped apricots, stir to combine and roast for a further 12 minutes until the vegetables are tender.
5. Garnish with fresh parsley, then serve with lemon wedges on the side.

STORE: Cool completely and seal the glass dish with the lid. Then store in the fridge for up to 3 days.

REHEAT: Remove the lid and attach the portable air fryer. Use the Recrisp function to heat for 6–7 minutes, or until hot, stirring halfway through.

PREP AND GO: To make this ahead of time, prep up to step 2, attach the lid and store in the fridge for up to 24 hours. Once ready to cook, attach to the portable air fryer and continue from step 3.

MEALS WITH MAX TIPS:
- For a spicier kick, add 1 teaspoon of harissa paste when seasoning the veg.
- Try swapping the apricots for raisins or chopped dates for a different sweetness.
- If you are cooking for one, halve the ingredients and cook this in the large dish.

● **Calories:** 480   ● **Protein:** 17g   ● **Carbs:** 85g   ● **Fat:** 10g

Why order in when you can make your favourites faster and lighter at home? These fakeaway recipes capture all the flavour, crunch and comfort of a takeaway – without breaking the bank. From Chinese classics like Sweet and Sour Chicken with Rice (page 130) to juicy burgers, they're made for nights when you want that same satisfaction, fresh from your own kitchen. The Loaded Beef Nachos (page 140) is one of my favourite recipes – cheesy, crunchy and everything you want from a fakeaway night in.

Sweet and Sour Chicken with Rice	130
Chicken Katsu Curry with Rice	132
Salt and Pepper Chicken	134
Hot Honey Chicken Burger	136
Crispy Bang-Bang Tofu Loaded Fries	138
Loaded Beef Nachos	140
Sweet Chilli Halloumi and Red Pepper Burger	142

Fakeaways

08

Sweet and Sour Chicken with Rice

SERVES 2
Cook time: 25 minutes

This classic fakeaway is all about that sticky, tangy sauce. The portable air fryer makes the chicken pieces golden and crisp before they get tossed in the sweet and sour glaze. Paired with fluffy rice, it's colourful, comforting and just as good as the takeaway – but lighter and fresher.

INGREDIENTS:
300g/10½oz chicken breast, diced
2 tbsp cornflour
2 tsp oil
120g/4oz rice
2 spring onions, thinly sliced
salt and black pepper

FOR THE SAUCE:
4 tbsp ketchup
1 tbsp rice vinegar
1 tbsp soy sauce
4 tbsp pineapple juice
2 tsp honey
2 garlic cloves, finely grated
2 tsp finely grated fresh ginger

METHOD:
1. Place the diced chicken into a bowl and mix with the cornflour, oil and a big pinch of salt and black pepper.
2. Add the chicken to the large glass dish of the Ninja Crispy, on top of the tray.
3. Air fry for 12–14 minutes. Flip halfway through the cooking time.
4. Meanwhile, cook the rice according to the packet instructions. If using microwave rice, heat this a few minutes before the dish is ready.
5. In a bowl, mix all the sauce ingredients together and add 4 tablespoons of water. Once the chicken is cooked, remove the tray and place the chicken directly into the bottom of the glass air fryer dish. Add the sauce and stir to coat, then air fry for a further 3 minutes until the sauce is sticky and glossy.
6. Divide the rice between two bowls, add the chicken and top with the spring onions.

STORE: Cool completely and seal the glass dish with the lid. Then store in the fridge for up to 3 days. Store the rice separately or cook it when ready to serve.

REHEAT: Remove the lid and attach the portable air fryer. Use the Recrisp function to heat for 6–7 minutes, or until hot. Cook or heat the rice separately as needed.

PREP AND GO: To make this ahead of time, prep up to step 2, attach the lid and store in the fridge for up to 3 days. Once ready to cook, attach to the portable air fryer and continue from step 3. You can prep the sauce in advance and store separately, if you like.

MEALS WITH MAX TIPS:
- After coating the chicken in cornflour, let it sit for a few minutes before frying. This helps it to crisp up better.
- Taste and adjust your sauce before adding to the dish – extra vinegar for more tang, honey for sweetness or even add some chilli flakes for heat.
- If you are cooking for one, halve the ingredients and cook this in the large dish.

Calories: 489 **Protein:** 52g **Carbs:** 64g **Fat:** 3g

Chicken Katsu Curry with Rice

Golden, crispy chicken with a rich, fragrant curry sauce – this is the kind of dish that always feels like a treat. It's simple to make at home and serving it with rice makes it a proper comfort bowl. I love this one when I want something hearty but still homemade.

SERVES 2

Cook time: 30 minutes

INGREDIENTS:
2 x 150g/5¼oz chicken breasts
2 tbsp plain flour
2 eggs, beaten
8 tbsp panko breadcrumbs
2 small carrots, roughly diced
1 onion, roughly diced
oil spray
80g/3oz rice
2 garlic cloves, thinly sliced
2 tsp thinly sliced fresh ginger
1 tsp curry powder
1 tsp ground turmeric
2 tsp soy sauce
2 tsp honey
200ml/7fl oz chicken stock
salt and black pepper
chopped coriander, to garnish

METHOD:
1. Butterfly the chicken breasts by slicing them in half lengthways, without slicing all the way through. Open out the chicken breasts – they should be flat and an even thickness. Season with salt and black pepper.
2. Place the flour in one bowl, beaten eggs in another bowl and breadcrumbs into a third bowl.
3. Coat the chicken in the flour, then in beaten egg, then in the breadcrumbs.
4. Place the diced carrots and onion into the bottom of the large glass dish of the portable air fryer without the tray, and spray with a little oil. Air fry for 8 minutes.
5. Place the tray on top of the veg, then put the chicken onto the tray. Spray with a little oil, then air fry for 14 minutes. Flip the chicken halfway through the cooking time.
6. Cook the rice according to the packet instructions.
7. While the rice cooks, remove the chicken from the air fryer and leave to rest for a couple of minutes.
8. Place the cooked vegetables into a blender, with the garlic, ginger, curry powder, turmeric, soy sauce, honey and hot chicken stock. Blend until smooth.
9. Divide the cooked rice between two plates and top with the crispy chicken. Spoon the sauce over the chicken and then garnish with some fresh coriander.

STORE: Cool completely, put the chicken back in the glass dish and seal with the lid. Then store in the fridge for up to 3 days. Store the sauce separately. Heat the rice when serving.

REHEAT: Remove the lid and attach the portable air fryer. Use the Recrisp function to heat for 6 minutes, or until hot. Heat the rice separately in the microwave. Reheat the sauce in a small saucepan or in the microwave.

MEALS WITH MAX TIPS:
- If the sauce is a little too thick, add a little more chicken stock.
- For a creamier sauce, you could add 1–2 tablespoons of coconut milk before blending.
- If you like it spicy, you could garnish with some sliced red chilli.
- If you are cooking for one, halve the ingredients and cook this in the large dish.
- You can use microwave rice to save time, if you want.

Calories: 497   **Protein:** 59g   **Carbs:** 49g   **Fat:** 8g

Salt and Pepper Chicken

This recipe takes the Chinese takeaway favourite and transforms it into something you can make at home with less oil but all the flavour. Crispy chicken tossed with peppers, onions, chilli and plenty of seasoning – it's salty, spicy and completely addictive. Perfect with rice, noodles or just on its own.

SERVES 2

Cook time: 25 minutes

INGREDIENTS:
- 2 x 150g/5 ¼oz chicken breasts
- 2 tbsp cornflour
- 2 tbsp plain flour
- 1 red pepper, sliced into strips
- 1 green pepper, sliced into strips
- 2 small onions, sliced
- oil spray
- 2 tsp Chinese five spice
- 2 tsp garlic granules
- 2 fresh red chillies, sliced
- 2 spring onions, sliced
- salt and black pepper

METHOD:
1. Slice the chicken breast into bite-sized pieces. Season with salt and black pepper.
2. In a bowl, mix the cornflour and plain flour. Toss the chicken pieces in the flour, mix until well coated and then set aside.
3. Place the peppers and onions directly into the bottom of the large glass dish of the portable air fryer, without the tray. Air fry for 8 minutes until soft.
4. Place the tray on top of the veg, then arrange the chicken on top of the tray. Spray lightly with oil.
5. Air fry for 12 minutes, flipping the chicken halfway through the cooking time. Spray the chicken with a little more oil after flipping.
6. Remove the tray and place the chicken into the bottom of the glass dish with the veg.
7. Sprinkle over the Chinese five spice, garlic granules and sliced red chillies. Spray with a little more oil and toss everything together until it is fully coated. Air fry for a further 2 minutes.
8. Sprinkle the sliced spring onions on top and then enjoy. Lovely!

STORE: Cool completely and seal the glass dish with the lid. Then store in the fridge for up to 3 days.

REHEAT: Remove the lid and attach the portable air fryer. Use the Recrisp function to heat for 6 minutes, or until hot.

MEALS WITH MAX TIPS:
- For extra crunch, you can cook the chicken for an extra couple of minutes before mixing with the veg.
- If you like it super-spicy, you can add some dried chilli flakes in with the seasonings for extra heat.
- If you are cooking for one, halve the ingredients and cook this in the large dish..

One Pot

Calories: 352 **Protein:** 59g **Carbs:** 21g **Fat:** 4g

Hot Honey Chicken Burger

SERVES 2

Cook time: 18 minutes

Spicy, sticky and sweet – this burger hits all the right notes. The portable air fryer gets the chicken crunchy on the outside and juicy on the inside, then it's drizzled with hot honey for that irresistible glaze. Stuffed into a bun, it's messy, fun and one of my go-tos for a weekend fakeaway.

INGREDIENTS:
2 x 150g/5¼oz chicken breasts
1 tsp smoked paprika
1 tsp garlic granules
oil spray
2 brioche burger buns
2 tbsp light mayonnaise
handful of lettuce leaves
½ tomato, sliced
salt and black pepper

FOR THE HOT HONEY GLAZE:
4 tsp honey
big pinch of chilli flakes
2 tsp apple cider vinegar

METHOD:
1. Butterfly the chicken breasts by slicing them in half lengthways, without slicing all the way through. Open out the chicken breasts – they should be flat and an even thickness. Season with salt, black pepper, the smoked paprika and garlic granules.
2. Place the chicken into the large glass dish of the portable air fryer, on top of the tray.
3. Spray lightly with oil and air fry for 10 minutes. Flip halfway through the cooking time.
4. In a small bowl, combine the hot honey glaze ingredients.
5. Brush the chicken with the hot honey glaze and air fry for a further 2 minutes until cooked through.
6. Toast the burger buns lightly in the air fryer for the last 2 minutes of cooking time.
7. Spread mayonnaise on the base bun, add lettuce and tomato slices, then top with the glazed chicken breast.
8. Serve immediately while the glaze is sticky and warm.

STORE: Cool the glazed chicken completely and seal the glass dish with the lid. Then store in the fridge for up to 3 days. Wait until you're ready to eat before building your burger.

REHEAT: Remove the lid and attach the portable air fryer. Use the Recrisp function to heat for 6–7 minutes, or until hot. Toast your bun and then build your burger!

PREP AND GO: To prep this ahead of time, prep up to step 2 and attach the lid. Store in the fridge for up to 24 hours. Once ready to cook, attach to the portable air fryer and continue from step 3.

MEALS WITH MAX TIPS:
- For a juicer burger, you can swap the chicken breast for chicken thighs. They are juicier and more flavourful, but higher in calories.
- For a smokier twist, you could add 1 teaspoon of chipotle paste to the glaze.
- If you are cooking for one, halve the ingredients and cook this in the large dish.

One Pot

Calories: 468   **Protein:** 60g   **Carbs:** 39g   **Fat:** 9g

PREP + GO

SERVES 2
Cook time: 35 minutes

INGREDIENTS:
400g/14oz Maris Piper potatoes, peeled
oil spray
360g/12½oz extra-firm tofu, pressed
2 tbsp cornflour
2 spring onions, thinly sliced
2 small red chillies, sliced
salt and black pepper

FOR THE BANG-BANG SAUCE:
3 tbsp light mayonnaise
2 tbsp sweet chilli sauce
2 tsp sriracha
1 tsp honey

Crispy Bang-Bang Tofu Loaded Fries

This dish is a proper crowd-pleaser. The tofu cooks up crisp and golden, then it's drizzled with creamy, spicy bang-bang sauce over a pile of fries. It's a great one to share, though you'll probably want the whole portion to yourself!

METHOD:

1. Cut the peeled potatoes into fries, about 1cm/½in thick. Place them into the large glass dish of the portable air fryer, on top of the tray, and spray with a little oil. Stir them and spray again to make sure they are all evenly coated. Season with some salt.
2. Air fry the fries for 14 minutes, stirring halfway through the cooking time.
3. Meanwhile, cut the pressed tofu into bite-sized cubes. Season with salt and black pepper, then toss in the cornflour until evenly coated.
4. After the fries have cooked for 14 minutes, push them to one side of the dish and add the tofu to the other side.
5. Spray the tofu lightly with oil. Air fry for a further 12–15 minutes, tossing halfway, until the fries are golden and the tofu is crisp.
6. While the tofu and fries cook, mix all bang-bang sauce ingredients in a small bowl until smooth.
7. Transfer the fries to a serving plate, top with the crispy tofu and drizzle generously with bang-bang sauce.
8. Top with the sliced spring onion and red chillies, then enjoy.

STORE: Cool completely and seal the glass dish with the lid. Then store in the fridge for up to 3 days. Store the sauce, spring onions and sliced chillies separately.

REHEAT: Remove the lid and attach the portable air fryer. Use the Recrisp function to heat for 6 minutes, or until hot and crispy. Serve with the sauce, spring onions and chillies.

MEALS WITH MAX TIPS:
- Add a squeeze of lime over the finished dish for freshness.
- Feel free to swap the tofu for cauliflower to mix it up!
- If you are cooking for one, halve the ingredients and cook this in the large dish.

One Pot

Calories: 486 **Protein:** 26g **Carbs:** 56g **Fat:** 18g

Loaded Beef Nachos

Nachos are the ultimate fakeaway, and this version is hearty and full of flavour. Crispy tortilla chips are loaded with spiced beef, melted cheese, salsa and soured cream – it's everything you want in comfort food. Perfect for sharing with friends, or halve the recipe and serve as a dinner-for-one treat.

SERVES 2

Cook time: 20 minutes

INGREDIENTS:
- 300g/10½oz 5% fat beef mince
- 1 small onion, finely diced
- 1 red pepper, finely diced
- 1 tsp ground cumin
- 1 tsp smoked paprika
- 1 tsp chilli powder
- oil spray
- 240g/8½oz lightly salted tortilla chips
- 120g/4oz light Cheddar, grated
- 6 tbsp salsa
- 2 tbsp jalapeños
- 2 tbsp light soured cream
- salt and black pepper
- chopped coriander, to garnish

METHOD:
1. Add the beef mince, diced onion and diced red pepper to the large glass dish of the portable air fryer, without the tray.
2. Season with the cumin, smoked paprika, chilli powder, salt and black pepper. Then spray with a little oil.
3. Air fry for 10–12 minutes, stirring halfway through the cooking time, until the beef is browned and cooked through.
4. Carefully remove from the dish and set aside. Then spread the tortilla chips evenly in the dish.
5. Spoon the cooked beef mixture over the top, then sprinkle with the grated cheese.
6. Air fry for 3–4 minutes until the cheese is melted and bubbling.
7. Remove from the air fryer and transfer to your serving plate. Top with the salsa, jalapeños and light soured cream. Garnish with chopped fresh coriander and enjoy.

STORE: Cool the beef mixture completely after step 3 and seal the glass dish with the lid. Then store in the fridge for up to 3 days. It's best to store this before adding the tortilla chips, otherwise they will go soggy.

REHEAT: Remove the lid and attach the portable air fryer. Use the Recrisp function to heat for 6 minutes, or until hot. Then continue from step 4.

MEALS WITH MAX TIPS:
- For extra crunch, air fry the tortilla chips for 1 minute before adding the beef and cheese.
- Add a handful of black beans with the beef for extra protein and fibre.
- If you are cooking for one, halve the ingredients and cook this in the large dish.

One Pot

Calories: 462 **Protein:** 52g **Carbs:** 32g **Fat:** 14g

Sweet Chilli Halloumi and Red Pepper Burger

Halloumi is always a winner, and here it's paired with roasted red pepper and a sweet chilli glaze for a veggie burger that's anything but boring. The portable air fryer gives the halloumi that golden crust, and the whole thing is packed into a soft bun for a seriously satisfying meal.

SERVES 2

Cook time: 20 minutes

INGREDIENTS:
- 1 red bell pepper
- oil spray
- 180g/6oz halloumi
- 2 tbsp sweet chilli sauce
- 2 burger buns, split
- handful of lettuce leaves
- 2 tbsp light mayonnaise

METHOD:
1. Slice the red pepper into a large flat piece. Add the red pepper slice to the glass dish of the portable air fryer, on top of the tray, and spray with a little oil.
2. Chop the block of halloumi in quarters to create four flat square pieces. Place the halloumi slices in the air fryer and spray with a little oil.
3. Air fry for 10 minutes, flipping halfway through the cooking time.
4. Brush the halloumi with sweet chilli sauce and air fry for 1 minute more to glaze.
5. Toast the burger buns in the air fryer for 1–2 minutes.
6. Build your burgers! Spread mayo on the bottom halves of the burger buns, then add the lettuce, red pepper, halloumi and then the tops of the buns. Serve hot and enjoy, lovely!

STORE: Cool the halloumi and peppers completely and seal the glass dish with the lid. Then store in the fridge for up to 3 days.

REHEAT: Remove the lid and attach the portable air fryer. Use the Recrisp function to heat for 5–6 minutes, or until hot. Then build your burgers.

PREP AND GO: To prep this ahead of time, follow the above instructions to the end of step 2 and then attach the storage lid. Store in the fridge for up to 3 days. Once ready to cook, attach to the portable air fryer and continue from step 3.

MEALS WITH MAX TIPS:
- For more heat, you could add some chilli flakes.
- For a less spicy version, swap the sweet chilli sauce for honey.
- For extra flavour, you could mix the mayonnaise with a squeeze of lemon juice and a pinch of garlic powder.
- If you are cooking for one, halve the ingredients and cook this in the smaller dish.

One Pot

Calories: 480 **Protein:** 19g **Carbs:** 37g **Fat:** 29g

Perfectly crispy snacks in minutes – that's the magic of the air fryer. Whether you're craving something savoury and salty or a quick bite between meals, these recipes deliver crunch without compromise. Most use just a handful of ingredients and cook faster than the oven can preheat. Ideal for parties, movie nights, or when hunger strikes. My favourite recipe from this section is the Crispy BBQ Chicken Wings with Ranch Dip (page 146) – smoky, tangy and so moreish you'll want to make a double batch.

Crispy BBQ Chicken Wings with Ranch Dip	146
Popcorn Chicken Bites	148
Sticky Korean Sesame Chicken Strips	150
Crispy Mozzarella Sticks with Marinara Sauce	152
Feta and Spinach Filo Parcels	154
Onion Bhajis with Raita	156
Crispy Roasted Chickpeas	158

Snacks

09

Crispy BBQ Chicken Wings with Ranch Dip

These wings are everything you want in a snack – crispy skin, smoky-sweet BBQ flavour and a cooling ranch dip on the side. They're messy and moreish; the kind of thing that disappears fast whenever I make them. Perfect for sharing, though I never want to!

SERVES 2

Cook time: 25 minutes

INGREDIENTS:
2 tbsp cornflour
1 tsp baking powder
360g/12½oz chicken wings
oil spray
4 tbsp BBQ sauce
salt and black pepper
finely chopped chives, to garnish

FOR THE RANCH DIP:
2 tbsp light mayonnaise
2 tbsp 0% fat Greek yogurt
2 tbsp milk
1 tsp garlic powder
1 tsp onion powder
1 tsp dried dill
1 tsp dried parsley
2 tsp white vinegar

METHOD:
1. In a bowl, mix the cornflour with the baking powder, a pinch of salt and some black pepper.
2. Pat the wings dry using kitchen paper. Once dry, coat the wings evenly in the dry mix.
3. Spray the wings lightly with some oil. Place the wings into the large glass dish of the portable air fryer, on the tray.
4. Air fry for 20 minutes, turning halfway through the cooking time.
5. In a mixing bowl, mix all the ranch dip ingredients together until fully combined. Season to taste with salt and pepper.
6. Once crispy, transfer the wings to a bowl, add the BBQ sauce and toss the wings until fully coated.
7. Serve the wings garnished with chives and with the ranch sauce on the side. Lovely!

STORE: Cool completely and seal the glass dish with the lid. Then store the wings in the fridge for up to 3 days.

REHEAT: Remove the lid and attach the portable air fryer. Use the Recrisp function to heat for 6 minutes, or until hot.

PREP AND GO: To prep this ahead of time, follow the above instructions to the end of step 3 and then attach the storage lid. Store in the fridge for up to 3 days. Once ready to cook, attach to the portable air fryer and continue from step 3. You can prep the ranch sauce and store this separately in the fridge for a few days.

MEALS WITH MAX TIPS:
- Be sure to pat the wings dry prior to coating – this ensures they get nice and crispy!
- Feel free to mix up the sauce. These work great with sweet chilli, teriyaki or buffalo sauce instead of the BBQ sauce.
- If you are cooking for one, halve the ingredients and cook this in the large dish.

One Pot

Calories: 465 **Protein:** 42g **Carbs:** 5g **Fat:** 31g

Popcorn Chicken Bites

Little bites of crispy chicken that are crunchy on the outside and tender inside – these are such a fun snack. They're great for dipping, piling into wraps or just eating by the handful. A lighter, homemade twist on the fast-food classic.

SERVES 2
Cook time: 22 minutes

INGREDIENTS:
60g/2oz plain flour
2 tsp salt
2 tsp ground black pepper
2 tsp garlic powder
2 tsp smoked paprika
2 eggs, beaten
80g/3oz panko breadcrumbs
400g/14oz chicken breast, cut into small bite-sized chunks
oil spray

METHOD:
1. In a small bowl, combine the flour with half of the salt, black pepper, garlic powder and paprika.
2. Put the eggs in another bowl.
3. Add the breadcrumbs to a third bowl and mix with the remaining salt, black pepper, garlic powder and paprika.
4. Slice the chicken into small bite-sized chunks. Coat each piece of chicken in the flour, then egg, then breadcrumbs. Press to coat well.
5. Insert the tray into the large glass dish of the portable air fryer then arrange the chicken bites in a single layer on the tray.
6. Spray the tops lightly with oil.
7. Air fry for 14 minutes, turning halfway through the cooking time, until golden and cooked through. Serve hot and enjoy!

STORE: Cool completely and seal the glass dish with the lid. Then store in the fridge for up to 3 days.

REHEAT: Remove the lid and attach the portable air fryer. Use the Recrisp function to heat for 6 minutes, or until hot.

PREP AND GO: To prep this ahead of time, follow the above instructions to the end of step 5 and then attach the storage lid. Store in the fridge for up to 24 hours. Once ready to cook, attach to the portable air fryer and continue from step 6, adding 1–2 minutes to the cook time as the chicken is cooking from chilled.

MEALS WITH MAX TIPS:
- Serve with a dip like sweet chilli, BBQ or ranch (see page 146).
- Add 2 tablespoons of grated Parmesan to the breadcrumb mix for an extra savoury kick.
- If you are cooking for one, halve the ingredients and cook this in the large dish.

One Pot

Calories: 358   **Protein:** 51g   **Carbs:** 18g   **Fat:** 8g

Sticky Korean Sesame Chicken Strips

These chicken strips are coated in a sticky, spicy-sweet sauce and finished with toasted sesame seeds. They've got a lovely balance of heat and sweetness, and the air fryer makes them perfectly golden before the glaze goes on. They're the kind of snack that keeps you going back for 'just one more'.

SERVES 2

Cook time: 25 minutes

INGREDIENTS:
- 40g/1½oz plain flour
- 1 tsp garlic powder
- 1 tsp salt
- 2 eggs, beaten
- 80g/3oz panko breadcrumbs
- 400g/14oz chicken breast, sliced into thin strips
- oil spray
- 2 tsp toasted sesame seeds
- 2 spring onions, thinly sliced

FOR THE KOREAN GLAZE:
- 2 tbsp honey
- 2 tbsp low-salt soy sauce
- 2 tsp gochujang
- 2 tsp rice vinegar or lime juice
- 1 tsp sesame oil
- 2 garlic cloves, finely grated
- 1 tsp finely grated fresh ginger

METHOD:
1. Mix the flour, garlic powder and salt in one bowl. Add the beaten eggs to another bowl. Then add the panko breadcrumbs to a third bowl.
2. Coat the chicken strips in the flour, then the egg and then the breadcrumbs. Press to coat well.
3. Insert the tray into the large glass dish of the portable air fryer, then arrange the chicken strips in a single layer on the tray.
4. Spray the tops lightly with oil.
5. Air fry 15 minutes, flipping halfway through the cooking time, until golden and cooked through.
6. While the chicken cooks, combine all the glaze ingredients in a small pan. Heat gently until it bubbles and thickens slightly, about 1–2 minutes.
7. When the chicken is done, toss gently with the warm glaze.
8. Sprinkle with sesame seeds and spring onions, then serve.

STORE: Cool the unglazed chicken completely and seal the glass dish with the lid. Then store in the fridge for up to 3 days. It's best to add the glaze just before eating.

REHEAT: Remove the lid and attach the portable air fryer. Use the Recrisp function to heat for 6 minutes, or until hot.

PREP AND GO: To prep this ahead of time, follow the above instructions to the end of step 3 and then attach the storage lid. Store in the fridge for up to 24 hours. Once ready to cook, attach to the portable air fryer and continue from step 4, adding 1–2 minutes to the cook time as the chicken is cooking from chilled.

MEALS WITH MAX TIPS:
- Serve over rice or in lettuce wraps for a full meal.
- Double the glaze, if you want, extra for dipping!
- If you are cooking for one, halve the ingredients and cook this in the large dish.

One Pot

Calories: 449   **Protein:** 51g   **Carbs:** 35g   **Fat:** 11g

Crispy Mozzarella Sticks with Marinara Sauce

This recipe is pure comfort food – gooey melted cheese wrapped in a crunchy coating, served with a rich marinara sauce for dipping. The mozzarella sticks cook beautifully, coming out golden and crisp without the need for a deep fat fryer. This is a proper crowd-pleaser for movie nights or parties.

SERVES 2

Cook time: 15 minutes

INGREDIENTS:
120g/4oz firm mozzarella
30g/1oz plain flour
2 eggs, beaten
60g/2oz panko breadcrumbs
1 tbsp grated Parmesan
2 tsp garlic powder
½ tsp dried oregano
oil spray
salt

FOR THE MARINARA DIP:
200g/7oz passata
1 tsp garlic granules
1 tsp dried oregano
big pinch of chilli flakes

METHOD:
1. Cut the mozzarella into 6–8 even sticks. Pat dry with kitchen paper to remove excess moisture.
2. Add the flour to one bowl, the beaten eggs to another and the breadcrumbs to a third bowl.
3. Mix the breadcrumbs with the Parmesan, garlic powder, oregano and a pinch of salt.
4. Coat the mozzarella sticks in the flour, then the eggs, then the breadcrumbs.
5. Place the breaded sticks on a small tray or plate and freeze for at least 1 hour – this is essential to stop the cheese from leaking out when cooking.
6. Insert the tray into the large glass dish of the portable air fryer then arrange the breaded mozzarella sticks on the tray. Spray lightly with oil.
7. Air fry for 8–10 minutes, flipping halfway through the cooking time, until golden and crisp. The cheese should be just melting.
8. While it cooks, warm the passata in a small saucepan with the garlic granules, oregano, chilli and a pinch of salt. Heat gently until thickened slightly.
9. Serve the mozzarella sticks with the marinara dip on the side.

STORE: Best served hot and fresh. Cooked sticks can be stored in the fridge for 1 day, but may lose their crispiness.

REHEAT: Remove the lid and attach the portable air fryer. Use the Recrisp function to heat for 2–3 minutes, or until hot and starting to melt.

PREP AND GO: To prep this ahead of time, follow the above instructions to the end of step 5 and then attach the storage lid. Freeze for up to 2 weeks, ready to cook straight from frozen from step 6.

MEALS WITH MAX TIPS:
- Feel free to mix it up and swap the marinara sauce for BBQ or ranch (see page 146)!
- For extra crunch, you can 'double dip' the mozzarella sticks! Once you've coated them, dip them back into the egg and then back into the breadcrumbs.
- If you are cooking for one, halve the ingredients and cook this in the smaller dish.

One Pot

Calories: 315 **Protein:** 16g **Carbs:** 19g **Fat:** 14g

Feta and Spinach Filo Parcels

Light, flaky, and full of flavour – these parcels are a brilliant veggie snack. The salty feta pairs perfectly with the spinach, and the filo pastry cooks up beautifully crisp in the air fryer. They look impressive but are surprisingly easy to make.

SERVES 2

Cook time: 18 minutes

INGREDIENTS:
100g/3½oz cooked spinach
80g/3oz feta, crumbled
2 small garlic cloves, grated
1 tsp dried oregano
2 sheets of filo pastry
2 tsp melted unsalted butter
black pepper

METHOD:
1. In a bowl, mix the cooked spinach, crumbled feta, garlic, oregano and a pinch of black pepper.
2. Lay the filo sheets on your chopping board and cut each one into two strips (widthways).
3. Place a spoonful of the filling near the bottom of each strip.
4. Fold the filo over the filling and roll into a rectangle, folding the sides in as you go.
5. Brush the outsides with melted butter.
6. Place the tray into the large glass dish of the portable air fryer, then lay the parcels seam-side down in a single layer on the tray.
7. Air fry for 10–12 minutes, flipping once if needed, until golden and crisp.
8. Allow to cool for a minute before serving.

STORE: Cool completely and seal the glass dish with the lid. Then store in the fridge for up to 3 days.

REHEAT: Remove the lid and attach the portable air fryer. Use the Recrisp function to heat for 4–5 minutes, or until hot.

MEALS WITH MAX TIPS:
- Drain that spinach! Press out as much liquid as possible or the filling will go soggy.
- Feel free to switch up the filling! Add chopped sun-dried tomatoes or cooked mushrooms for extra flavour.
- If you are cooking for one, halve the ingredients and cook this in the large dish.

One Pot

Calories: 257   **Protein:** 13g   **Carbs:** 29g   **Fat:** 11g

Onion Bhajis with Raita

Crispy, spiced onion bhajis are such a treat, and they cook perfectly in the portable air fryer. Paired with a cooling raita, they're fragrant, crunchy and packed with flavour. Great as a snack, starter, or even part of a bigger Indian-style spread.

SERVES 2

Cook time: 20 minutes

INGREDIENTS:
1 large onion, thinly sliced
50g/1¾oz gram flour (chickpea flour)
½ tsp cumin seeds
½ tsp ground coriander
½ tsp ground turmeric
½ tsp chilli powder (optional)
½ tsp salt
½ tsp baking powder
2 tbsp chopped coriander
oil spray

FOR THE RAITA:
80g/3oz Greek yogurt
50g/1¾oz cucumber, grated and squeezed dry
2 tsp chopped mint
big pinch of ground cumin
salt and black pepper

METHOD:

1. Add the sliced onions to a bowl. Then sprinkle over the gram flour, spices, salt, baking powder and chopped coriander.
2. Mix well with your hands; the onions will start to release some moisture.
3. Add 4 teaspoons of water, a little at a time, until it forms a sticky coating around the onions. Add more water if needed, but you don't want it too runny.
4. Place the tray into the large glass dish of the portable air fryer, then spoon the mixture onto the tray, forming six small mounds.
5. Press gently to flatten slightly and then spray the tops with oil.
6. Air fry for 10–12 minutes, flipping halfway through the cooking time, until crisp and golden.
7. Meanwhile, make the raita. Mix the yogurt, grated cucumber, mint, cumin and a pinch of salt and black pepper in a small bowl.
8. Allow the onion bhajis to cool for a minute, then serve with the raita on the side. Lovely!

STORE: Cool completely and seal the glass dish with the lid. Then store the bhajis in the fridge for up to 3 days. Store the raita separately in the fridge.

REHEAT: Remove the lid and attach the portable air fryer. Use the Recrisp function to heat for 4–5 minutes until hot and crispy again.

MEALS WITH MAX TIPS:
- Add 1 teaspoon of garam masala for a deeper flavour and some chilli powder for spice!
- Don't overcrowd the dish – give the bhajis room to crisp up properly.
- If you are cooking for one, halve the ingredients and cook this in the smaller dish.

One Pot

Calories: 167   **Protein:** 8g   **Carbs:** 24g   **Fat:** 6g

Crispy Roasted Chickpeas

PREP + GO

SERVES 2
Cook time: 15 minutes

These are one of my favourite healthy snacks – crunchy, salty and endlessly customisable. Toss them with your favourite spices, crisp them up in the portable air fryer and you've got an addictive snack that's high in protein and fibre. Perfect for nibbling or sprinkling over salads.

INGREDIENTS:
- 400g/14oz drained tinned chickpeas, rinsed
- 2 tsp olive oil
- 1 tsp garlic powder
- ½ tsp smoked paprika
- ½ tsp ground cumin
- salt

METHOD:
1. Pat the chickpeas dry using a clean tea towel or kitchen paper. Remove any loose skins for extra crispness.
2. Add the chickpeas to a bowl. Then toss with the oil, spices and a big pinch of salt until evenly coated.
3. Insert the tray into the large glass dish of the portable air fryer. Add the chickpeas and spread them out into an even layer on the tray.
4. Air fry for 12–15 minutes, shaking or stirring every 5 minutes, until golden and crispy.
5. Let the chickpeas cool for 5–10 minutes – they will crisp up as they cool. Then serve and enjoy. Lovely!

STORE: Cool completely and seal the glass dish with the lid. Then store at room temperature for up to 2 days.

REHEAT: These do not need reheating, enjoy any time! If you want, you can warm them through on the Recrisp setting for 1–2 minutes to make them extra crispy.

PREP AND GO: To prep this ahead of time, follow the above instructions to the end of step 3 and then attach the storage lid. Store in the fridge for up to 24 hours. Once ready to cook, attach to the portable air fryer and continue from step 4.

MEALS WITH MAX TIPS:
- Make sure you dry the chickpeas thoroughly. Moisture = soggy chickpeas, which nobody wants!
- Add lemon zest and finely chopped fresh rosemary for a Mediterranean twist, or some chilli powder for spice.
- If you are cooking for one, halve the ingredients and cook this in the smaller dish.

One Pot

Calories: 292   **Protein:** 16g   **Carbs:** 45g   **Fat:** 6g

Dessert in the air fryer? Absolutely. From gooey chocolate cakes to golden fruit crumbles, these recipes prove that portable air fryers like the Ninja Crispi aren't just for savoury food. Most can be made in one dish with minimal mess. Keep an eye on timing – desserts can go from perfect to overdone quickly – and enjoy them warm, straight from the fryer. The Chocolate Lava Cake (page 164) is one of my go-to desserts – rich, molten and the ultimate way to end any meal.

Mini Peanut Butter Cookies	162
Chocolate Lava Cake	164
Chocolate Brownie Bites	166
Carrot Cake Muffins	168
Cinnamon Oat Apple Crumble	170
Caramelised Pears with Walnuts	172
Berry Oat Bars	174

Sweet Treats

10

SERVES 2

Cook time: 10 minutes

INGREDIENTS:
75g/2¾oz peanut butter
4 tbsp honey
25g/1oz plain flour
½ tsp vanilla extract
salt

Mini Peanut Butter Cookies

These little cookies are dangerously moreish. They are crisp on the outside, soft in the middle and full of peanut butter flavour. They take only minutes to cook in the portable air fryer, and I love making a batch to keep on hand for when I fancy something sweet with a cup of tea.

METHOD:
1. Add all the ingredients to a mixing bowl and mix until fully combined.
2. Divide into four equal portions and then individually roll them in your hands to form four balls.
3. Using a fork, press down on top of each ball to squash it down a little, then rotate the fork 90 degrees and press down again. This should give you a flat cookie shape with a crisscross pattern on top. Repeat this process with all the balls.
4. Place into the small glass dish of the portable air fryer, on top of the tray.
5. Air fry for 6 minutes, or until golden brown.
6. Allow to cool before removing from the air fryer.

STORE: Cool completely and seal the glass dish with the lid. Then store in the fridge for up to 3 days.

REHEAT: These do not need reheating, enjoy any time!

PREP AND GO: To prep this ahead of time, follow the above instructions to the end of step 4 and then attach the storage lid. Store in the fridge for up to 3 days. Once ready to cook, attach to the portable air fryer and continue from step 5.

MEALS WITH MAX TIPS:
- Add chopped dark chocolate for mini choc chip cookies.
- Keep an eye them after 4–5 minutes as they can burn quickly.

One Pot

Calories: 287   **Protein:** 8g   **Carbs:** 27g   **Fat:** 17g

Chocolate Lava Cake

This recipe feels like pure indulgence: a rich, gooey centre hidden inside a soft chocolate sponge. It's the kind of dessert that looks impressive but is surprisingly easy to pull off. Perfect for when you want a quick chocolate fix that feels restaurant-worthy.

SERVES 2

Cook time: 12 minutes

INGREDIENTS:
50g/1¾oz dark chocolate
40g/1½oz unsalted butter
1 egg
1 egg yolk
30g/1oz caster sugar
20g/¾oz plain flour
salt
butter, for greasing
cocoa powder, for dusting
icing sugar, for dusting

METHOD:

1. Melt the chocolate and butter together in the microwave or in a saucepan over a low heat.
2. In a bowl, whisk the egg, egg yolk and sugar until light and fluffy.
3. Pour in the melted chocolate mixture and stir to combine. Gently fold in the flour and a pinch of salt.
4. Grease your ramekin (or a mug) with butter and lightly dust with cocoa powder.
5. Spoon the batter into your ramekin. Then air fry for 8–10 minutes until just set on the outside.
6. Leave to cool for a minute, then gently run a knife around the outside of the cake. Place a plate on top and flip it upside down. Tap the top of the ramekin to loosen the cake and then carefully lift the ramekin off.
7. Dust with icing sugar, then cut in half and serve immediately.

STORE: Cool completely and seal the glass dish with the lid. Then store in the fridge for up to 3 days.

REHEAT: These do not need reheating, enjoy any time! You can warm them through for a couple of minutes if you prefer.

MEALS WITH MAX TIPS:

- For best results, use one ramekin instead of two. The cake will likely be too flat otherwise. You can have a larger serving to yourself or cut in half after cooking to divide into the two portions.
- This tastes amazing served with vanilla ice cream or custard! For a healthier option, you could add a dollop of Greek yogurt.

Calories: 405 **Protein:** 6g **Carbs:** 30g **Fat:** 29g

Chocolate Brownie Bites

These brownie bites are fudgy, chocolatey and the perfect size for snacking. The portable air fryer cooks them beautifully, so you get a crisp edge with a soft middle. I love serving them warm with a little scoop of ice cream, but they're just as good straight from the fridge.

SERVES 2

Cook time: 25 minutes

INGREDIENTS:
100g/3½oz dark chocolate
60g/2oz unsalted butter, plus extra for greasing
2 eggs
80g/3oz caster sugar
1 tsp vanilla extract
40g/1½oz plain flour
1 tbsp cocoa powder
salt
icing sugar, for dusting

METHOD:
1. Melt the chocolate and butter together in the microwave or in a small pan over a low heat.
2. In a bowl, beat the eggs and sugar until slightly foamy and thickened.
3. Gradually add the chocolate mixture to the bowl with the eggs and sugar, stirring continuously. Then stir through the vanilla extract.
4. Sift in the plain flour and cocoa powder. Then add a pinch of salt. Fold the mixture until its fully combined and smooth, but don't overmix.
5. Lightly grease the small glass dish of the portable air fryer with some butter, then pour in the brownie mixture.
6. Cook on the Roast setting for 15-17 minutes until the brownie is set on top and slightly wobbly in the middle.
7. Cool completely in the dish, then slice into small squares. Dust with icing sugar before serving, then enjoy!

STORE: Cool completely and seal the glass dish with the lid. Then store in the fridge for up to 3 days.

REHEAT: These do not need reheating, enjoy any time! You can warm them through for a couple of minutes if you prefer.

MEALS WITH MAX TIPS:
- Don't try to remove the brownies from the dish as soon as they've finished cooking. Let them cool completely. They firm up as they cool down.
- Want some extra texture? You could add some finely chopped walnuts to the mixture.

Calories: 374 **Protein:** 7g **Carbs:** 19g **Fat:** 31g

PREP + GO

SERVES 2
Cook time: 20 minutes

INGREDIENTS:
1 egg
60g/2oz soft brown sugar or coconut sugar
2 tbsp honey or maple syrup
60g/2oz unsalted butter, melted
½ tsp vanilla extract
1 carrot, finely grated
120g/4oz plain flour
45g/1½oz rolled oats
1 tsp baking powder
1 tsp ground cinnamon
pinch of ground nutmeg
20g/¾oz raisins or chopped walnuts (optional)
salt

Carrot Cake Muffins

All the flavours of a classic carrot cake, but in a lighter, grab-and-go muffin. They're warmly spiced, naturally sweet and finished with a soft texture that keeps them moist. These are one of my favourite bakes for meal prep – they make breakfast or snacking feel special.

METHOD:
1. In a bowl, whisk the egg, sugar, honey, melted butter and vanilla until smooth.
2. Stir in the grated carrot.
3. In a separate bowl, combine the flour, oats, baking powder, cinnamon, nutmeg and a pinch of salt.
4. Fold the dry ingredients into the wet until fully combined. Add the raisins or nuts, if using.
5. Divide the mixture among 6–8 silicone muffin moulds and place in the large glass dish of the portable air fryer.
6. Air fry for 12–14 minutes until the top is set and a skewer comes out mostly clean.
7. Allow to cool before serving, then enjoy. Lovely!

STORE: Cool completely and seal the glass dish with the lid. Then store in the fridge for up to 3 days.

REHEAT: These do not need reheating, enjoy any time! You can warm them through for a couple of minutes if you prefer.

PREP AND GO: To prep this ahead of time, follow the above instructions to the end of step 4 and then store the batter in an airtight container. Store in the fridge for up to 2 days. Once ready to cook, continue from step 5.

MEALS WITH MAX TIPS:
- Add orange zest to the batter for a fresh twist.
- Top with a light cream cheese glaze after cooling; this will increase the calories, but it's tasty!
- You can use dark brown or light brown sugar - use dark brown sugar for a deeper flavour and colour.

One Pot

Calories: 241   **Protein:** 4g   **Carbs:** 35g   **Fat:** 9g

Cinnamon Oat Apple Crumble

This crumble is pure comfort in a bowl. Sweet baked apples topped with a crunchy cinnamon oat layer – it's simple, wholesome and feels like autumn in every bite. I often make it when I want a dessert that feels a little lighter.

SERVES 3

Cook time: 22 minutes

INGREDIENTS:
3 apples, peeled and chopped
4 tsp honey
1 tsp lemon juice
1 tsp ground cinnamon

FOR THE TOPPING:
65g/2¼oz rolled oats
30g/1oz plain flour
½ tsp ground cinnamon, for topping
30g/1oz unsalted butter, cold and cut into cubes
30g/1oz honey, for topping
salt

METHOD:
1. Mix the apple with the honey, lemon juice, cinnamon and 2 tablespoons of water.
2. Add the apple mixture to the small glass dish of the portable air fryer, without the tray.
3. Air fry for 6–7 minutes until the apples start to soften, then stir them.
4. For the topping, in a bowl, mix the oats, flour, cinnamon and a pinch of salt. Rub in the butter until crumbly. Then stir in the honey.
5. Sprinkle the crumble topping over the softened apples.
6. Air fry for 8–10 minutes until the topping is golden and crisp.
7. Let it cool slightly before serving, then enjoy.

STORE: Cool completely and seal the glass dish with the lid. Then store in the fridge for up to 3 days.

REHEAT: You can eat this cold, but it's better reheated! Use the Recrisp function and reheat for 3–4 minutes.

MEALS WITH MAX TIPS:
- For extra crunch, add chopped walnuts or flaked almonds to the topping.
- Serve warm with yogurt or custard, or eat cold from the fridge.

One Pot

Calories: 346   **Protein:** 4g   **Carbs:** 64g   **Fat:** 10g

Caramelised Pears with Walnuts

This is one of the simplest but most elegant desserts in the book. The portable air fryer caramelises the pears until golden and soft, then they're topped with crunchy walnuts for texture. It's the perfect way to end a meal without being too heavy.

SERVES 2

Cook time: 15 minutes

INGREDIENTS:
- 2 ripe pears, peeled, halved and cored
- 2 tbsp honey
- 1 tsp ground cinnamon
- 6 tbsp Greek yogurt
- 2 tbsp walnuts, chopped
- 2 tsp chocolate sauce

METHOD:
1. Place the pear halves, cut-side up, into the large glass dish of the portable air fryer, on top of the tray.
2. Drizzle the pears with the honey and sprinkle with the cinnamon.
3. Air fry for 10–12 minutes until soft and caramelised.
4. Spoon the Greek yogurt onto two plates or bowls and spread it into a circle. Place the warm, caramelised pears on top. Sprinkle with the chopped walnuts, then drizzle on the chocolate sauce.

STORE: Cool the pears completely and seal the glass dish with the lid. Then store in the fridge for up to 3 days. Store the yogurt, walnuts and chocolate sauce separately.

REHEAT: Remove the lid and attach the portable air fryer. Use the Recrisp function to heat for 4–5 minutes, or until warm, then serve with the yogurt, walnuts and chocolate sauce.

MEALS WITH MAX TIPS:
- For a more indulgent dessert, you could swap the Greek yogurt for some vanilla ice cream.
- Instead of shop-bought chocolate sauce, you could melt some dark chocolate and drizzle that on top instead!
- If you are cooking for one, halve the ingredients and cook this in the smaller tray.

One Pot

Calories: 276 **Protein:** 10g **Carbs:** 33g **Fat:** 11g

Berry Oat Bars

PREP + GO

SERVES 4
Cook time: 15 minutes

INGREDIENTS:
140g/5oz rolled oats
60g/2oz plain flour
pinch of salt
7 tsp honey or maple syrup
50g/1¾oz unsalted butter, melted
1 tsp vanilla extract
150g/5¼oz mixed berries, fresh or frozen

These fruity, chewy bars are just the right amount of sweet. The oats make them hearty, while the berries add a burst of freshness. They're brilliant for an evening sweet treat or breakfast on the go, and I also love having one as an afternoon snack with a cup of tea.

METHOD:
1. In a bowl, mix the oats, flour, salt, honey, melted butter and vanilla until crumbly and sticky.
2. Line the small glass dish of the portable air fryer with baking paper.
3. Firmly press two-thirds of the mixture into the dish to form a compact base layer.
4. Evenly scatter the berries over the base.
5. Crumble the remaining oat mixture over the top and gently press it down, so that it holds together but still looks rustic.
6. Cook on the Roast setting for 12–13 minutes until golden brown and just set.
7. Let it cool completely in the dish; this will help it firm up a bit. Then cut into four chunky bars.

STORE: Cool completely and seal the glass dish with the lid. Then store in the fridge for up to 3 days.

REHEAT: No need to reheat, but a 1-minute blast in the air fryer can bring back the freshly baked feel.

PREP AND GO: To prep this ahead of time, follow the above instructions to the end of step 5 and then attach the storage lid. Store in the fridge for up to 3 days. Once ready to cook, continue from step 6.

MEALS WITH MAX TIPS:
- Add grated orange zest for a citrusy flavour or a few chopped nuts for texture.
- For jammy berries, mash half of them before layering.

One Pot

Calories: 316   **Protein:** 6g   **Carbs:** 46g   **Fat:** 12g

Conversion Tables

WEIGHT

METRIC	IMPERIAL
15g	½oz
25g	1oz
40g	1½oz
50g	2oz
75g	3oz
100g	4oz
150g	5oz
175g	6oz
200g	7oz
225g	8oz
250g	9oz
275g	10oz
350g	12oz
375g	13oz
400g	14oz
425g	15oz
450g	1lb
550g	1¼lb
675g	1½lb
900g	2lb
1.5kg	3lb

VOLUME

METRIC	IMPERIAL
25ml	1fl oz
50ml	2fl oz
85ml	3fl oz
150ml	5fl oz (¼ pint)
300ml	10fl oz (½ pint)
450ml	15fl oz (¾ pint)
600ml	1 pint
700ml	1¼ pints
900ml	1½ pints
1 litre	1¾ pints

Index

A

apples
    apple pie baked oats 18
    cinnamon oat apple crumble 170
apricots: Moroccan-spiced veg tray with chickpeas and apricots 126
aubergines: ratatouille traybake with halloumi and balsamic glaze 102
avocados
    avocado, halloumi and tomato sourdough toast 30
    Mexican chicken burrito bowl 44
    smoky paprika prawn salad bowl 92
    spicy black bean quesadillas with guacamole and salsa 120

B

bacon and egg breakfast bites 28
baked ricotta and spinach pasta with a crispy cheesy crust 106
BBQ jackfruit wrap with slaw and pickles 114
BBQ pork tacos with coleslaw 72
beef
    beef and mushroom stroganoff traybake 60
    beef kofta salad with spiced chickpeas and mint yogurt sauce 50
    crispy chilli beef with rice 58
    Greek beef meatballs with courgette, feta and lemon rice 54
    loaded beef nachos 140
    Mexican beef and black bean tacos 52
    Philly cheesesteak bake with peppers and sweet potato wedges 62
    steak chimichurri bowl with crispy potatoes 56
berries
    berry oat bars 174
    cinnamon French toast with frozen berries and yogurt 20
black beans
    Mexican beef and black bean tacos 52
    spicy black bean quesadillas with guacamole and salsa 120

broccoli
    miso pork with sesame broccoli
        and rice 78
    sticky teriyaki chicken with broccoli
        and noodles 36
burgers
    hot honey chicken burger 136
    sweet chilli halloumi and red pepper
        burger 142

C

cabbage *see* red cabbage; white
    cabbage
Cajun cod with spinach, roasted
    peppers and turmeric rice 86
caramelised pears with walnuts 172
carrots
    BBQ jackfruit wrap with slaw and
        pickles 114
    BBQ pork tacos with coleslaw 72
    carrot cake muffins 168
    chicken katsu curry with rice 132
    Moroccan-spiced veg tray with
        chickpeas and apricots 126
    sausage and veg traybake with
        a sticky maple glaze 70
cauliflower: lemon roasted cauliflower
    salad with pomegranate and tahini
    dressing 118
Cheddar
    bacon and egg breakfast bites 28
    Italian tuna melt pasta bake 84
    loaded beef nachos 140
    Mexican beef and black bean
        tacos 52
    Philly cheesesteak bake with
        peppers and sweet potato
        wedges 62
cheese
    sausage and cheese breakfast
        muffin 22
    see also Cheddar; goat's cheese;
        halloumi; mozzarella; paneer;
        Parmesan; ricotta; vegan cheese;
        vegetarian hard cheese

chicken
    chicken katsu curry with rice 132
    crispy BBQ chicken wings with ranch
        dip 146
    harissa chicken with chickpeas,
        courgette and crispy potatoes 34
    hot honey chicken burger 136
    Italian chicken parmigiana salad 40
    lemon garlic chicken thighs
        with green beans and baby
        potatoes 42
    Mexican chicken burrito bowl 44
    popcorn chicken bites 148
    salt and pepper chicken 134
    sticky Korean sesame chicken
        strips 150
    sticky teriyaki chicken with broccoli
        and noodles 36
    sweet and sour chicken with
        rice 130
    sweet chilli chicken flat bread 46
    Thai-inspired chicken satay with
        rice 38
chickpeas
    beef kofta salad with spiced
        chickpeas and mint yogurt
        sauce 50
    crispy chickpea and sweet
        potato salad 116
    crispy roasted chickpeas 158
    falafel wrap with pickled red
        onion and garlic yogurt 98
    harissa chicken with chickpeas,
        courgette and crispy
        potatoes 34
    Moroccan-spiced veg tray with
        chickpeas and apricots 126
chilli-lemon salmon with corn salsa
    and zesty rice 94
chocolate brownie bites 166
chocolate lava cake 164
chorizo and sweet potato hash 26
cinnamon French toast with frozen
    berries and yogurt 20
cinnamon oat apple crumble 170

coconut milk
    Thai green cod traybake 82
    tofu, sweet potato and spinach curry bake 124
cod
    Cajun cod with spinach, roasted peppers and turmeric rice 86
    Thai green cod traybake 82
cookies: mini peanut butter cookies 162
coriander: Indian paneer and pepper bake with coriander chutney 104
courgettes
    courgette, red onion and goat's cheese frittata 24
    Greek beef meatballs with courgette, feta and lemon rice 54
    harissa chicken with chickpeas, courgette and crispy potatoes 34
    Moroccan-spiced veg tray with chickpeas and apricots 126
    pesto pork with courgette and cherry tomatoes 76
    ratatouille traybake with halloumi and balsamic glaze 102
    Thai green cod traybake 82
crispy bang-bang tofu loaded fries 138
crispy BBQ chicken wings with ranch dip 146
crispy cheesy veggie quesadilla 100
crispy chickpea and sweet potato salad 116
crispy chilli beef with rice 58
crispy gnocchi with tomatoes and pesto 108
crispy mozzarella sticks with marinara sauce 152
crispy roasted chickpeas 158
crispy salmon fishcakes with cucumber salad and mint yogurt 90
cucumbers
    beef kofta salad with spiced chickpeas and mint yogurt sauce 50
    crispy chickpea and sweet potato salad 116
    crispy salmon fishcakes with cucumber salad and mint yogurt 90
    falafel wrap with pickled red onion and garlic yogurt 98
    Greek pork gyros with tzatziki 68
    lemon roasted cauliflower salad with pomegranate and tahini dressing 118
    onion bhajis with raita 156
    smoky paprika prawn salad bowl 92

E

edamame beans: teriyaki tofu bowl with edamame and rice 122
eggs
    apple pie baked oats 18
    bacon and egg breakfast bites 28
    chicken katsu curry with rice 132
    chorizo and sweet potato hash 26
    cinnamon French toast with frozen berries and yogurt 20
    courgette, red onion and goat's cheese frittata 24
    crispy mozzarella sticks with marinara sauce 152
    crispy salmon fishcakes with cucumber salad and mint yogurt 90
    Italian chicken parmigiana salad 40
    popcorn chicken bites 148
    sticky Korean sesame chicken strips 150

F

falafel wrap with pickled red onion and garlic yogurt 98
fennel: Italian style pork and fennel meatballs with spaghetti 66

INDEX

feta
- cherry tomato, feta and basil pasta bake 110
- feta and spinach filo parcels 154
- Greek beef meatballs with courgette, feta and lemon rice 54
- pesto pork with courgette and cherry tomatoes 76

filo pastry: feta and spinach filo parcels 154

fish *see* cod; king prawns; salmon; tuna

flatbreads
- Greek pork gyros with tzatziki 68
- sweet chilli chicken flat bread 46

G

garlic and rosemary pork chops with baby potatoes 74

gnocchi: crispy gnocchi with tomatoes and pesto 108

goat's cheese: courgette, red onion and goat's cheese frittata 24

Greek beef meatballs with courgette, feta and lemon rice 54

Greek pork gyros with tzatziki 68

Greek yogurt
- apple pie baked oats 18
- beef kofta salad with spiced chickpeas and mint yogurt sauce 50
- Cajun cod with spinach, roasted peppers and turmeric rice 86
- caramelised pears with walnuts 172
- cherry tomato, feta and basil pasta bake 110
- cinnamon French toast with frozen berries and yogurt 20
- crispy BBQ chicken wings with ranch dip 146
- crispy chickpea and sweet potato salad 116
- crispy salmon fishcakes with cucumber salad and mint yogurt 90

falafel wrap with pickled red onion and garlic yogurt 98

Greek beef meatballs with courgette, feta and lemon rice 54

Greek pork gyros with tzatziki 68

Indian paneer and pepper bake with coriander chutney 104

lemon roasted cauliflower salad with pomegranate and tahini dressing 118

onion bhajis with raita 156

prawn tacos with mango salsa and lime yogurt 88

smoky paprika prawn salad bowl 92

sweet chilli chicken flat bread 46

green beans
- garlic and rosemary pork chops with baby potatoes 74
- lemon garlic chicken thighs with green beans and baby potatoes 42

green peppers
- Philly cheesesteak bake with peppers and sweet potato wedges 62
- salt and pepper chicken 134

H

halloumi
- avocado, halloumi and tomato sourdough toast 30
- ratatouille traybake with halloumi and balsamic glaze 102
- sweet chilli halloumi and red pepper burger 142

harissa chicken with chickpeas, courgette and crispy potatoes 34

hot honey chicken burger 136

I

Indian paneer and pepper bake with coriander chutney 104
Italian chicken parmigiana salad 40
Italian style pork and fennel meatballs with spaghetti 66
Italian tuna melt pasta bake 84

J

jackfruit: BBQ jackfruit wrap with slaw and pickles 114

K

king prawns
　prawn tacos with mango salsa and lime yogurt 88
　smoky paprika prawn salad bowl 92

L

lemon
　chilli-lemon salmon with corn salsa and zesty rice 94
　Greek beef meatballs with courgette, feta and lemon rice 54
　lemon garlic chicken thighs with green beans and baby potatoes 42
　lemon roasted cauliflower salad with pomegranate and tahini dressing 118
lettuce leaves
　hot honey chicken burger 136
　sweet chilli halloumi and red pepper burger 142
lime: prawn tacos with mango salsa and lime yogurt 88
loaded beef nachos 140

M

mangoes: prawn tacos with mango salsa and lime yogurt 88
Mexican beef and black bean tacos 52
Mexican chicken burrito bowl 44
mini peanut butter cookies 162
miso pork with sesame broccoli and rice 78
Moroccan-spiced veg tray with chickpeas and apricots 126
mozzarella
　baked ricotta and spinach pasta with a crispy cheesy crust 106
　crispy cheesy veggie quesadilla 100
　crispy mozzarella sticks with marinara sauce 152
　Italian chicken parmigiana salad 40
　Italian tuna melt pasta bake 84
　Philly cheesesteak bake with peppers and sweet potato wedges 62
muffins
　carrot cake muffins 168
　sausage and cheese breakfast muffin 22
mushrooms: beef and mushroom stroganoff traybake 60

N

noodles: sticky teriyaki chicken with broccoli and noodles 36

O

oats
　apple pie baked oats 18
　berry oat bars 174
　carrot cake muffins 168
　cinnamon oat apple crumble 170
onions
　chicken katsu curry with rice 132
　crispy cheesy veggie quesadilla 100

INDEX

loaded beef nachos 140
onion bhajis with raita 156
salt and pepper chicken 134
tofu, sweet potato and spinach curry bake 124
see also red onions

P

paneer: Indian paneer and pepper bake with coriander chutney 104
panko breadcrumbs
  chicken katsu curry with rice 132
  crispy mozzarella sticks with marinara sauce 152
  Italian chicken parmigiana salad 40
  popcorn chicken bites 148
  sticky Korean sesame chicken strips 150
Parmesan
  baked ricotta and spinach pasta with a crispy cheesy crust 106
  cherry tomato, feta and basil pasta bake 110
  crispy gnocchi with tomatoes and pesto 108
  crispy mozzarella sticks with marinara sauce 152
  Italian chicken parmigiana salad 40
  Italian style pork and fennel meatballs with spaghetti 66
passata
  cherry tomato, feta and basil pasta bake 110
  crispy mozzarella sticks with marinara sauce 152
  Indian paneer and pepper bake with coriander chutney 104
  Italian chicken parmigiana salad 40
  Italian style pork and fennel meatballs with spaghetti 66

pasta
  baked ricotta and spinach pasta with a crispy cheesy crust 106
  beef and mushroom stroganoff traybake 60
  fusilli pasta, cherry tomato, feta and basil pasta bake 110
  Italian style pork and fennel meatballs with spaghetti 66
  Italian tuna melt pasta bake 84
peanut butter: mini peanut butter cookies 162
pears: caramelised pears with walnuts 172
pesto pork with courgette and cherry tomatoes 76
Philly cheesesteak bake with peppers and sweet potato wedges 62
pomegranate seeds: lemon roasted cauliflower salad with pomegranate and popcorn chicken bites 148
pork
  BBQ pork tacos with coleslaw 72
  garlic and rosemary pork chops with baby potatoes 74
  Greek pork gyros with tzatziki 68
  Italian style pork and fennel meatballs with spaghetti 66
  miso pork with sesame broccoli and rice 78
  pesto pork with courgette and cherry tomatoes 76
  see also sausages
potatoes
  crispy bang-bang tofu loaded fries 138
  crispy salmon fishcakes with cucumber salad and mint yogurt 90
  garlic and rosemary pork chops with baby potatoes 74
  harissa chicken with chickpeas, courgette and crispy potatoes 34

lemon garlic chicken thighs
with green beans and baby
potatoes 42
sausage and veg traybake with
a sticky maple glaze 70
steak chimichurri bowl with
crispy potatoes 56
Thai green cod traybake 82
prawns *see* king prawns

R

ratatouille traybake with halloumi and
balsamic glaze 102
red cabbage: BBQ jackfruit wrap with
slaw and pickles 114
red onions
    beef and mushroom stroganoff
traybake 60
    beef kofta salad with spiced
chickpeas and mint yogurt
sauce 50
    chilli-lemon salmon with corn salsa
and zesty rice 94
    courgette, red onion and goat's
cheese frittata 24
    crispy chickpea and sweet potato
salad 116
    falafel wrap with pickled red onion
and garlic yogurt 98
    Greek beef meatballs with
courgette, feta and lemon rice 54
    Greek pork gyros with tzatziki 68
    Indian paneer and pepper bake
with coriander chutney 104
    Italian chicken parmigiana
salad 40
    Mexican beef and black bean
tacos 52
    Mexican chicken burrito bowl 44
    Moroccan-spiced veg tray with
chickpeas and apricots 126
    Philly cheesesteak bake with
peppers and sweet potato
wedges 62
    prawn tacos with mango salsa
and lime yogurt 88
    ratatouille traybake with halloumi
and balsamic glaze 102
    sausage and veg traybake with
a sticky maple glaze 70
    smoky paprika prawn salad bowl 92
    spicy black bean quesadillas with
guacamole and salsa 120
    sweet chilli chicken flat bread 46
red peppers
    Cajun cod with spinach, roasted
peppers and turmeric rice 86
    chorizo and sweet potato hash 26
    crispy cheesy veggie quesadilla 100
    crispy chilli beef with rice 58
    Indian paneer and pepper bake with
coriander chutney 104
    loaded beef nachos 140
    Mexican chicken burrito bowl 44
    Moroccan-spiced veg tray with
chickpeas and apricots 126
    Philly cheesesteak bake with
peppers and sweet potato
wedges 62
    ratatouille traybake with halloumi
and balsamic glaze 102
    salt and pepper chicken 134
    sausage and veg traybake with
a sticky maple glaze 70
    sweet chilli halloumi and red pepper
burger 142
    Thai green cod traybake 82
rice
    Cajun cod with spinach, roasted
peppers and turmeric rice 86
    chicken katsu curry with rice 132
    chilli-lemon salmon with corn salsa
and zesty rice 94
    crispy chilli beef with rice 58
    Greek beef meatballs with
courgette, feta and lemon rice 54
    Mexican chicken burrito bowl 44
    miso pork with sesame broccoli
and rice 78

INDEX

smoky paprika prawn salad bowl 92
sweet and sour chicken with rice 130
teriyaki tofu bowl with edamame and rice 122
Thai-inspired chicken satay with rice 38

ricotta
    baked ricotta and spinach pasta with a crispy cheesy crust 106
    crispy cheesy veggie quesadilla 100

S

salad leaves
    beef kofta salad with spiced chickpeas and mint yogurt sauce 50
    crispy chickpea and sweet potato salad 116
    falafel wrap with pickled red onion and garlic yogurt 98
    Italian chicken parmigiana salad 40
    lemon roasted cauliflower salad with pomegranate and tahini dressing 118
    kofta salad with spiced chickpeas and mint yogurt sauce 50

salads
    beef kofta salad with spiced chickpeas and mint yogurt sauce 50
    crispy chickpea and sweet potato salad 116
    crispy salmon fishcakes with cucumber salad and mint yogurt 90
    Italian chicken parmigiana salad 40
    lemon roasted cauliflower salad with pomegranate and tahini dressing 118
    smoky paprika prawn salad bowl 92

salmon
    chilli-lemon salmon with corn salsa and zesty rice 94
    crispy salmon fishcakes with cucumber salad and mint yogurt 90

salt and pepper chicken 134

sausages
    sausage and cheese breakfast muffin 22
    sausage and veg traybake with a sticky maple glaze 70

sesame seeds
    miso pork with sesame broccoli and rice 78
    sticky Korean sesame chicken strips 150
    sticky teriyaki chicken with broccoli and noodles 36
    teriyaki tofu bowl with edamame and rice 122

smoky paprika prawn salad bowl 92
spicy black bean quesadillas with guacamole and salsa 120

spinach
    baked ricotta and spinach pasta with a crispy cheesy crust 106
    Cajun cod with spinach, roasted peppers and turmeric rice 86
    chorizo and sweet potato hash 26
    courgette, red onion and goat's cheese frittata 24
    crispy cheesy veggie quesadilla 100
    feta and spinach filo parcels 154
    tofu, sweet potato and spinach curry bake 124

steak chimichurri bowl with crispy potatoes 56
sticky Korean sesame chicken strips 150
sticky teriyaki chicken with broccoli and noodles 36
sweet and sour chicken with rice 130
sweet chilli chicken flat bread 46

sweet chilli halloumi and red pepper
  burger 142
sweet potatoes
  chorizo and sweet potato hash 26
  crispy chickpea and sweet
    potato salad 116
  Moroccan-spiced veg tray with
    chickpeas and apricots 126
  Philly cheesesteak bake with
    peppers and sweet potato
    wedges 62
  tofu, sweet potato and spinach
    curry bake 124
sweetcorn
  chilli-lemon salmon with corn
    salsa and zesty rice 94
  Italian tuna melt pasta bake 84

T

tahini: lemon roasted cauliflower
  salad with pomegranate and tahini
  dressing 118
teriyaki tofu bowl with edamame
  and rice 122
Thai green cod traybake 82
Thai-inspired chicken satay with
  rice 38
tofu
  crispy bang-bang tofu loaded
    fries 138
  teriyaki tofu bowl with edamame
    and rice 122
  tofu, sweet potato and spinach
    curry bake 124
tomatoes, fresh
  avocado, halloumi and tomato
    sourdough toast 30
  beef kofta salad with spiced
    chickpeas and mint yogurt
    sauce 50
  cherry tomato, feta and basil
    pasta bake 110
  chilli-lemon salmon with corn
    salsa and zesty rice 94
crispy chickpea and sweet
  potato salad 116
crispy gnocchi with tomatoes
  and pesto 108
falafel wrap with pickled red
  onion and garlic yogurt 98
Greek pork gyros with tzatziki 68
hot honey chicken burger 136
Italian chicken parmigiana
  salad 40
Mexican chicken burrito bowl 44
pesto pork with courgette and
  cherry tomatoes 76
ratatouille traybake with halloumi
  and balsamic glaze 102
smoky paprika prawn salad
  bowl 92
spicy black bean quesadillas with
  guacamole and salsa 120
sweet chilli chicken flat bread 46
tofu, sweet potato and spinach
  curry bake 124
tomatoes, tinned
  Italian tuna melt pasta bake 84
  Moroccan-spiced veg tray with
    chickpeas and apricots 126
tortilla chips: loaded beef
  nachos 140
tortillas
  BBQ jackfruit wrap with slaw and
    pickles 114
  BBQ pork tacos with coleslaw 72
  crispy cheesy veggie
    quesadilla 100
  falafel wrap with pickled red onion
    and garlic yogurt 98
  Mexican beef and black bean
    tacos 52
  prawn tacos with mango salsa
    and lime yogurt 88
  spicy black bean quesadillas
    with guacamole and salsa 120
tuna: Italian tuna melt pasta
  bake 84

V

vegan cheese: spicy black bean quesadillas with guacamole and salsa 120

vegetarian hard cheese
baked ricotta and spinach pasta with a crispy cheesy crust 106
cherry tomato, feta and basil pasta bake 110
crispy gnocchi with tomatoes and pesto 108

W

walnuts: caramelised pears with walnuts 172

white cabbage: BBQ pork tacos with coleslaw 72

Y

yellow peppers
Cajun cod with spinach, roasted peppers and turmeric rice 86
Indian paneer and pepper bake with coriander chutney 104

About the Author

Max McCann is on a mission to make cooking simple, fun and stress-free. With over 2.5 million followers and more than 30 million monthly viewers across social media, he's become one of the internet's go-to food creators for quick, flavour-packed recipes. Known online as @MealsWithMax, Max never uses fussy ingredients or complicated steps – just real food that tastes amazing. In his debut cookbook, he takes that same approach off-screen, bringing together brand-new recipes designed to make everyday cooking easier, tastier and more enjoyable for everyone.

Acknowledgements

Watching this book come together has been one of the most rewarding experiences of my life. From writing and testing recipes, to getting feedback from my loved ones – mainly my fiancée **Rachel** – to seeing it all take shape through the photo shoots and design, it's been incredible watching so many moving parts slowly build into something real.

To **Steph Milner**, thank you for believing in me and in this idea, and for helping make it happen.

To **Samuel Heaton**, my editor – you've been patient, sharp and endlessly supportive. You've made this process a true collaboration, and I've loved every step.

To **Catherine Ngwong**, thank you for keeping everything running so smoothly behind the scenes and making the process feel easy when I know it wasn't.

To **Studio Polka**, your design work brings so much life and personality to these pages. You've captured exactly how I hoped this book would feel.

To **Clare Winfield**, your photography is stunning – you've made every dish look just as good as it tastes.

To **Troy Willis** and **Jessica Geddes**, thank you for the care, skill and calm energy you brought to every shoot. Working with you was an absolute joy.

To **Louie Waller**, thank you for adding that extra bit of character to every shot – the little details that make all the difference.

And to everyone who's cooked along with me, supported my recipes, or shared them with friends – you're the reason I get to do this. I hope this book inspires you to cook, experiment and enjoy the process as much as I do.

With huge thanks,
Max

EBURY PRESS

UK | USA | Canada | Ireland | Australia
India | New Zealand | South Africa

Ebury Press is part of the Penguin Random House group of companies whose addresses can be found at global.penguinrandomhouse.com

Penguin Random House UK
One Embassy Gardens, 8 Viaduct Gardens,
London SW11 7BW

penguin.co.uk
global.penguinrandomhouse.com

First published by Ebury Press in 2026
1

Copyright © Max McCann 2026
Photography © Clare Winfield 2026

The moral right of the author has been asserted.

Penguin Random House values and supports copyright. Copyright fuels creativity, encourages diverse voices, promotes freedom of expression and supports a vibrant culture. Thank you for purchasing an authorised edition of this book and for respecting intellectual property laws by not reproducing, scanning or distributing any part of it by any means without permission. You are supporting authors and enabling Penguin Random House to continue to publish books for everyone. No part of this book may be used or reproduced in any manner for the purpose of training artificial intelligence technologies or systems. In accordance with Article 4(3) of the DSM Directive 2019/790, Penguin Random House expressly reserves this work from the text and data mining exception.

Publishing Director: Steph Milner
Editor: Samuel Heaton
Production Controller: Catherine Ngwong
Designer: Studio Polka
Photographer: Clare Winfield
Food Stylist: Troy Willis, with Jessica Geddes
Prop Stylist: Louie Waller

Colour origination by Altaimage Ltd
Printed and bound in Italy by LEGO SpA

The authorised representative in the EEA is Penguin Random House Ireland, Morrison Chambers, 32 Nassau Street, Dublin D02 YH68.

A CIP catalogue record for this book is available from the British Library

ISBN 9781529981070

This book is independently published and not affiliated with or endorsed by SharkNinja Operating LLC or its related trade marks. NINJA CRISPI is a trade mark of SharkNinja Operating LLC. This book is independently published and not affiliated with or endorsed by SharkNinja Operating LLC or its related trade marks. NINJA CRISPI is a trade mark of SharkNinja Operating LLC.

Penguin Random House is committed to a sustainable future for our business, our readers and our planet. This book is made from Forest Stewardship Council® certified paper.